RAISING CHICKENS FOR BEGINNERS 2024

BACKYARD POULTRY FOR THE AMERICAN PATRIOT

KYLE DONOVAN

CONTENTS

EXCLUSIVE GIFT FOR MY READERS

Hello, Kyle Donovan here.

Your support of my work means the world to me. As a token of gratitude, I'm offering you a free ebook: "Survival Kits 101: Assemble, Adapt, Survive."

Link: https://bit.ly/SurvivalKitsFreeGiftBook

This guide will help you craft your personalized survival kit, regardless of your experience level, with detailed advice on gear selection and survival psychology.

Scan this QR code to download your free ebook:

Thanks for being a part of our prepared and resilient community.

Best,

Kyle Donovan

DOWNLOAD THE AUDIO VERSION OF THIS BOOK FREE

If you love listening to audiobooks on-the-go or would enjoy a narration as you read along, I have great news for you. You can download the audiobook version of *Raising Chickens for Beginners 2024* for FREE (Regularly $14.95) just by signing up for a FREE 30-day

Audible trial!

Scan the QR codes below to get started:

AUDIBLE US	GET THIS FOR FREE!	AUDIBLE UK

INTRODUCTION

The only way to make sense out of change is to plunge into it, move with it, and join the dance. –Alan Watts

There has never been a time when our world has changed so quickly. Most people find change scary, and even more so when it's so drastic. Whether we like it or not, things in our world will never be the same again, and we need to get used to this new normal. Recent world events such as the Russo-Ukrainian war, the global COVID-19 pandemic, and the uncertain economic state in which we find ourselves daily have led to many people turning back to the basics—self-sustainability.

Ukraine is one of the world's largest grain exporters, and not being able to export its grain as usual has led to an ever-growing hunger crisis in many countries that are dependent on it. This affected the entire agricultural economy, and even things like the availability of animal feed have been impacted. Both the war and the pandemic have caused massive economic problems and continue to do so.

All of these things affect us in our daily lives—much more than we might realize. Being self-sustainable has never been as important as in this day and age. The problem that we face is that we don't know how to grow our own crops and raise our own animals for food, so when push comes to shove, the ones who do will be in control.

A few years ago, we would have never imagined that the world would be in the state that it is today. This just goes to show how unpredictable the future is, and further demonstrates why it's important to learn new skills and adapt to our ever-changing environment.

Being self-sustainable gives the control back to the citizens. You don't have to rely on an uncertain future. Things can change at any moment. As Benjamin Franklin said, "Failing to prepare means you prepare to fail." Preparing for the worst in order to protect their families and themselves is the motivation behind becoming self-sustainable for most preppers.

But what about someone who is not a prepper? Should they also be concerned about becoming more self-sustainable? The answer is a very simple *yes*! Commercial farming is not only detrimental to the environment, but the quality of meat and other agricultural products that we get from it is questionable.

Commercial chicken farms have been known to feed their chickens unnecessary antibiotics and hormones to make them grow faster. As you can imagine, this is not very good for your health. By raising your own chickens, you know what they've been eating exactly, and you're able to take control back into your hands.

Everyone deserves to have their basic food needs met without having to rely on others. It is a common misconception that we can trust commercial farms with our food supply blindly. In fact, in most cases, we, as consumers, have no idea what goes into the production of that food. By buying from large commercial farms, we're putting money in the pockets of big corporations that care more about making a profit than about our health.

Raising your own chickens for meat and eggs is a great way to start working toward your self-reliance and self-sustainability. There is no limit to what you can do to become more self-reliant. The possibilities are endless. Raising chickens is but one part of it. Chicken farming is an extremely rewarding project, and throughout this book, it'll become clear to you why it is gaining popularity so fast.

In this book, you can expect to learn the basics of raising your own chickens. Whatever your motivation behind it may be, you'll find everything you need to make a success of this project. It can be done on a farm, plot, smallholding, or even your backyard! By learning this skill, you'll be practicing a more eco-friendly way of producing food. The excitement is endless, so let's get right into it!

CHAPTER 1
BASICS OF RAISING CHICKENS

Everyone wants to be strong and self-sufficient, but few are willing to put in the work necessary to achieve worthy goals. –Mahatma Gandhi

Whatever the motivation behind your endeavor may be, there are many reasons why raising your own chickens is beneficial. We'll be looking into those reasons, as well as some of the basics you need to know before starting your project.

WHY RAISE CHICKENS?

Anything worth doing has to hold some benefits Right? The benefits of chicken farming go far beyond the meat and eggs we eat on a daily basis. Raising your own chickens has many advantages, but the most important is what you stand to gain personally from it. The first and most important thing that comes to mind for me, is my health and my family's.

Health

Commercial chicken farms often keep their chickens in atrocious conditions. They are often cramped in spaces so small that it's impossible for them to even turn around. Since recent world events, we've all learned too well what that means. Diseases spread extremely fast, and E. coli and salmonella are bacteria that thrive in these conditions.

On top of that, not only are chickens fed all kinds of hormones and antibiotics to make them grow faster, but some chicken feed has even been found to contain an arsenic-based additive in the past to increase growth rate and pigment (American Chemical Society, 2007). Note that *arsenic* is "an extremely hazardous chemical that has been known to cause cancer and other serious health problems in humans."

Perhaps we have come a long way since arsenic made its way into our plates, or have we? The addition of this additive to certain poultry feeds has been reported as recently as 2018 (Pendergrass, 2018). While it has been banned in some countries, others still actively add it without remorse, claiming that it helps fight parasites in the chickens (Wiley, 2017).

You might be wondering why all of this disturbing information is necessary. The point is, the moment we raise our own chickens is the moment we say no to all of these dangerous chemicals and the degradation of our health that it causes. We have no idea what the long-term side effects of half of these additives are, but yet we trust commercial farms enough to feed them to us.

Commercial chicken farms are focused on fast and large production. This means that the feed is specially designed to make chickens grow faster than they're supposed to. Now, you can imagine that this feed doesn't contain all the nutrients to keep a growing chicken strong and healthy.

Organically farmed chickens are often fed a variety of nutrient-rich foods which hold much more benefits when consumed. This naturally leads to organically farmed products having a higher nutritional value than commercially farmed products. You get so much more out of one egg or piece of meat in this way.

Self-raised chickens contain more unsaturated fatty acids. Saturated fatty acids cause a variety of health problems, including cholesterol and heart disease, whereas unsaturated fats decrease the risk of these conditions. Organic eggs have also been proven to contain more vitamins and omega-3.

Chicken farming helps you take control of your health and know exactly what you're putting into your body. By choosing to take on this project, you're not only choosing to protect your health from harmful substances but potentially even increase it by eating foods with a higher nutritional value.

Gratification

Whether you're planning on starting a massive poultry project on a farm, perhaps keeping a few hens in the backyard for the daily breakfast egg, or even keeping some chickens as pets, chicken farming can be challenging. Our brains have been wired to seek out these challenges and overcome them because we're always looking for that gratification.

Overcoming some of the obstacles that come with chicken farming is an amazing feeling, especially if you put in a lot of hard work. To say that you gain a sense of accomplishment is an understatement! Knowing that you're providing your family with a healthier food option is a fantastic feeling.

Chicken farming literally allows you to see the fruits of your labor. If you manage it right, you'll get something in return in the form of eggs or meat. Your flock will grow, and your animals will become healthy, wonderful creatures that fill you with serenity. I always say there is nothing more beautiful than a healthy, happy animal. Seeing them thrive is one of the most rewarding things you'll experience when taking on this project.

You wouldn't believe it, but chickens actually make great pets as well. They're quite intelligent and can keep you busy. They're much less maintenance than many other pets, and they give you something in return, which is a big bonus. I've always found it quite peaceful to watch them go about their daily activities.

Information is priceless, and so are skills. These are the two things that can never be taken away from you, no matter what. You're learning a very important new skill by raising chickens and broadening your general knowledge in the process. You'll also be learning heaps about hard work and responsibility.

Chicken farming is the perfect opportunity to teach children these lessons and skills. They will be able to use what they've learned in this project for the rest of their lives. Even adults will benefit greatly from this, as I believe it's never too late to teach an old dog new tricks.

You haven't known gratification until you've eaten your own produce. There is nothing better than knowing that all of the hard work that you've put into your backyard chicken farming project has paid off and produced something extremely useful. The moment you eat that first home-produced egg or cook and eat that first roast chicken is something that you will remember for the rest of your life.

The Environment

Commercial broiler houses use a massive amount of energy and resources. As we all know, we have to be conscious of the impact our practices have on the environment. Higher energy usage is never good, as this is not sustainable.

Furthermore, commercial broiler houses are often cooled down by large electric fans and warmed up by electric heating systems. They also use synthetic light, which contributes to the total energy usage. Not only that but machinery that runs on fuel is often used to clean large broiler houses.

These big corporations try everything they can to keep diseases from spreading from one flock to the next, so they use many harmful chemicals to clean out these broiler houses.

At the end of the day, this is not sustainable. We're just pumping more and more chemicals and harmful greenhouse gasses into the atmosphere. Organic chicken farming is very different and much more sustainable. First of all, chemical usage is kept to a minimum, which means less harmful substances in the atmosphere.

There are countless different ways to implement organic chicken farming, but it will always include some form of free range and movement for the chickens. Many organic chicken farmers will move the enclosures around. This ensures that the chickens don't *overuse* a single area. Their droppings will fertilize the areas where they are moved, and the environment is protected and improved.

Moreover, the use of large machinery is usually kept to a minimum, which reduces fuel emissions. Chickens have access to natural light and are kept in generally more humane conditions. The animals are happier and healthier, which is always a big bonus. Even though we farm chickens for our personal gain in the form of meat and eggs, it should always be done in an ethical way toward the animals and the environment. Organic chicken farming will always seek to promote healthy biodiversity and soil health.

Commercial poultry farming enterprises ship their products all over, and if we really think about it, the amount of fossil fuels burned in the process is astonishing. Locally producing and selling your own food reduces your carbon footprint.

Backyard chicken farming can be done in a sustainable and regenerative way; instead of breaking down nature's resources, we give some of them back. If every family had their own backyard chicken farming project or even a quarter of all of the families in the United States, we would see a massive change in the environment around us. Regenerative farming is going to be the future, and I can't wait to see how we breathe back life into our atmosphere.

Economic Benefits

Whether you plan on raising chickens for your personal use or business, there are many economic benefits in doing so. If you plan on selling your produce, the economic benefit is obvious. Selling fresh eggs, for instance, will ensure that you always have a little extra in your pocket.

Perhaps you would like to mainly raise chickens for your own use but wouldn't mind selling the extra produce. This is a great way of saving money, as you can put the profit from selling the excess product right back into your project. Imagine your freshly produced, healthy product, starting to pay for itself! Organically produced food will generally sell for a much higher price, which means you'll gain a bigger profit by using a sustainable farming model.

On the other hand, chicken manure is known to be a fantastic fertilizer. If you have a garden of your own, you'll be saving money on fertilizer. If you don't, you can easily sell your fertilizer, as chicken manure is well sought after in the gardening community. In addition, chickens are handy helpers in the garden, as they eat many unwanted pests, such as snails and grasshoppers. This can save you a few dollars on pest management in the garden, as well as reduce the amount of chemicals you need to use.

As I've mentioned earlier, organic products are more expensive than commercially produced ones. You'll be saving a lot of money by producing your own organic products that are free of harmful chemicals rather than buying the same product in the supermarket.

The price of food is constantly rising. There is no stopping inflation, but we can adapt. By doing things like feeding your chickens kitchen scraps, you can save money on feed, which means saving even more money on your product. Availability of poultry can change in stores, but by raising your own chickens, you're guaranteed your eggs and meat according to your flock size.

Money has a way of controlling people and their behaviors. Just take your life as an example. Since food prices have risen so dramatically in the past few years, I can guarantee that your spending patterns have changed as well. If we can produce our own meat and eggs, we're taking back the economic power that these corporations have over us. They no longer get to influence the way we spend our money in that regard, and we get to make the choice ourselves.

If you produce a fresh product that the people in your area can buy from you, you keep wealth circulating locally instead of putting money in the pockets of big corporations. The money you make from locally selling your products doesn't only benefit you but everyone else in your area where you spend it again!

Independence

When it comes to independence, raising chickens is a gold mine. Chicken meat is a fantastic source of protein, containing many of the fats and nutrients we need to keep our bodies healthy. Not only that but chickens also produce eggs, of which an egg white is considered to be nearly 100% protein.

In order to be able to claim independence in any area of your life, you will have to be capable of filling the gap yourself. By raising chickens that produce such a high-quality product, you can improve your resilience and self-reliance.

The truth is the market is quite unpredictable, especially in our current economic climate. We don't know when a food shortage will hit or when the demand for poultry products will become too high for the produced amount. The availability of agricultural products hangs in a delicate balance far more intricate than we might think.

By raising your own chickens, you're guaranteed availability, and you don't have to rely on larger corporations to meet your needs in that aspect. You can also produce your fertilizer independently, reducing the amount of chemicals and synthetic products you use in your garden. We should also be thinking of the economic independence that we gain in this facet of our lives when raising our chickens.

The bottom line is that chicken farming has many benefits. Between the personal, environmental, and economic benefits, it's hard to imagine why one wouldn't want to do it. The truth is, apart from all of these great benefits, raising chickens is a very joyful experience. Even through the challenges that you may face, it will all be worth it in the end.

CHOOSING THE RIGHT CHICKENS FOR YOUR HOMESTEAD

Choosing the right breed for your project can be quite daunting, as there are literally thousands of breeds to choose from. In this section, we'll be looking at some popular breeds and their characteristics, as well as a few considerations you may want to think about when choosing the breed for your homestead.

When choosing your breed, there are a few questions that you should ask yourself. Chicken breeds can be categorized into three categories—broilers, layers, and dual-purpose breeds. *Broiler chickens* are "chickens mainly raised for meat production. In most cases, they have been carefully selected and bred to produce more meat of a better quality."

You will find that broilers are more often than not, larger breeds with more muscles than layer-breeds. This is because their sole purpose is to provide us with as much meat as possible while still being able to live a quality life. Once again, the difference between organic chicken farming and commercial chicken farming when it comes to broilers is clear. Commercial farms overcrowd and over-feed broilers, sometimes to the point where they get seriously injured or are no longer able to stand up due to their heavy weight and underdeveloped bones.

Layer breeds are specifically bred to lay more eggs at a higher quality. They can lay up to 300 eggs a year, whereas other breeds may average around half of that amount or more. Different layer breeds will produce different–looking eggs. Some eggs are white, others are brown, and you can even raise breeds that lay colorful or unusual eggs. The average egg size you get from your layers will also depend on the breed. There are differences within the breed, but most breeds have a relatively stable average size.

Dual-purpose breeds have been selected and bred to perform well in both the meat and egg production categories. These breeds can be used for one of these purposes or even both. Many dual-purpose breeds perform at the top of both categories, such as the Rhode Island Red. Some have even speculated that their meat tastes better than other breeds. Note that many factors can have an influence on the taste of the product, and the breed is definitely one of them.

In order to decide on the breed that you should get, you should think about your goals:

- Do you want to produce eggs, meat, or both?
- What is your preference for egg size and color?
- How much do you need to produce?

Once you've figured out the end goal of this project, you'll be able to steer yourself in the right direction. This will tell you whether you should get layers, broilers, or dual-purpose breeds. With this out of the way, you're one step closer to choosing the perfect breed.

The space you have available should also be taken into consideration. If you plan on starting your project on a farm or somewhere where you have a lot of space available, you don't really have to worry about the size of the breed. However, if you want to raise chickens in your backyard and you don't have a lot of space available, you might want to consider getting a smaller breed. There are variations in sizes in all three of the breed categories.

Just like with any other animals, certain breeds are better suited to certain climates. For instance, Australorps are a chicken breed that handles cold weather very well. Even though they can also tolerate a warm climate, they're best suited for colder weather. On the other hand, breeds that have large combs or smaller bodies may be more susceptible to frostbite and will require extra heating during colder times. It is generally easier for larger breeds to adapt to cold climates.

Breeds that have small wattles, feathered feet, or short legs won't be suitable for hot climates. This is because they don't have enough surface area where heat may escape from. Some breeds have thick feather coats, which will also make living in a warm climate unpleasant and sometimes even dangerous for them.

Thus, before deciding on a breed, always ensure that you have done sufficient research on their climate preferences. For breeds that are not well-suited to your climate, you may have to invest some extra time and money in preparing the coop for them, such as adding additional heat for breeds that do not do well in cold climates.

This will also mean that you'll be using more energy to make things tolerable for them. The best option remains picking a breed that is perfectly suited to your environment. This will save you a lot of energy, worry, and money in the long run.

Different chicken breeds have different temperaments. Some breeds are quite docile and unbothered, whereas others may become aggressive. There are also breeds which are a mix between the two. Consider your goals when deciding on getting a docile, aggressive, or mixed breed.

If you plan on keeping your chickens in a very intimate homestead or backyard where you'll constantly be in contact with them, getting an aggressive breed may pose problems. Chickens have a very sophisticated hierarchy in their flocks, and they constantly compete with each other for the higher rank.

Keeping aggressive breeds in small spaces will definitely increase their aggression toward you and other flock members. Aggressive breeds do best in larger spaces. Docile breeds are ideal for smaller spaces. Even if a breed is known as docile, they will still compete with each other for their place in the hierarchy; however, it prob-ably won't be as violent or frequent as with aggressive breeds.

If you have enough space and you don't handle your flock too often, you can consider getting an aggressive breed. Aggressive breeds are better at protecting each other from predators as well. If you decide to do this, ensure that you do research on how to handle aggression from your chickens.

If you have children who come into contact with your chickens, aggressive breeds are definitely out. Roosters can do immense damage and even send a child to the hospital. Even though chickens are smaller than us, we should never underestimate their power and agility. Between their claws and beaks, you really don't want to take a chance.

To summarize everything, here are the main points to take into consideration when choosing a breed:

- What do you want to produce?
- How much do you want to produce?
- How much space do you have available?
- Climate characteristics and suitable breeds for your region.
- Breed temperament.

POPULAR BREEDS AND THEIR CHARACTERISTICS

Now that you know what you should think about before choosing a breed, we'll be going over a few popular breeds and their characteristics, which may help you make a choice.

Cornish Cross

The Cornish Cross chicken is "a mixture of the Cornish chicken and a White Rock chicken. This hybrid is known for its outstanding meat production and exceptionally fast growth." Where other broilers are slaughtered at around 10–12 weeks, the Cornish Cross is ready to be slaughtered between 8 and 10 weeks (*The Cornish Cross Chicken*, 2022).

The Cornish Cross is usually raised in larger farming settings and even commercial broiler houses. This chicken breed has shown record growth and is widely popular. It is white all over and can weigh up to 6 lbs upon slaughter (Robin, 2021).

The important thing to know about this breed is that they aren't a good breeding breed, which means you will most likely have to buy them as chicks, raise them, slaughter them, and then buy the next flock. They're also not hardy chickens, and you may encounter some challenges when it comes to keeping their environment ideal for them.

If you plan on doing a totally free-range system, this is not the breed for you. We'll be looking into different chicken housing options in the next section of this chapter. The Cornish Cross doesn't look for food like other breeds, and if they don't have enough space, they will become overweight and unhealthy very fast.

Their temperament is relatively docile, and they won't give you any problems in terms of aggression. If you plan on raising a large number of chickens and you have the facilities for it, the Cornish Cross might be a good option. However, they are quite a tricky breed to raise, and I wouldn't recommend them for the total beginner.

Overall, this breed produces a lot, and it produces fast, but I wouldn't recommend it to the homesteader. There are just too many issues with keeping it happy and healthy, and unless you're farming with it on a large scale, it's just not worth it. Even though the fast production is an advantage, this breed is basically the *pug* of chickens. It has been bred to fulfill a specific role, but at what cost? These chickens have to be slaughtered at the right age, or they will become so obese that it would be cruel to keep them in such a state.

Big Red Broiler

These red chickens are almost the opposite of the Cornish Cross, except when it comes to production. The Big Red Broiler has been bred for high meat production, and they do very well in homesteading settings. They're great foragers and will easily adapt to a free-range system.

They will mature and grow fast, but not as fast as the Cornish Cross. You can expect them to mature at around 12 weeks and can even weigh up to 10 lbs by that time (Davis, 2022).

The challenge associated with this breed is, once again, reproduction. They don't reproduce well and will also have to be bought per flock. The Red Ranger is considered a *previous version* of the Big Red Broiler, breed and they share many of the same characteristics, down to their hardiness when it comes to hot and cold weather.

Furthermore, this breed won't give you health issues like some other broiler breeds, and they're a good breed to start with if you're considering raising chickens only for meat. They lay brown eggs, but if you're looking to raise chickens for eggs or meat and eggs, there are better-suited breeds out there. However, for the sole purpose of meat, you can't go wrong with this breed.

There is one major concern when it comes to the Big Red Broiler, and that is its temperament. They have been known to be quite an aggressive breed, so they won't be well suited for homesteads with small children or in situations where you are in constant contact with your chickens. These most definitely don't make good pets.

Leghorn

Although there are quite a few different types of Leghorns on the market, we'll be looking at the white Leghorn specifically. The Leghorn is an extremely popular layer breed all over the world, and it's not hard to imagine why. Compared to other breeds, they have a massive egg production potential and require less food to produce eggs.

Leghorns are well suited for warmer climates due to their large combs and will require additional heating during colder seasons. They produce white, large eggs, and can produce up to 320 eggs per year (Conde, 2023). Leghorns are very well suited for free-ranging, as they're excellent foragers.

With layer breeds, we generally don't want our hens to go *broody*, meaning that they want to sit on the eggs in order for them to hatch. The Leghorn is known for its non-broodiness, which is an advantage in the layer industry.

They will do well on a homestead; however, if you want to breed with them, you will most likely need to incubate the eggs artificially. Leghorns are highly fertile and an overall great breed. They don't produce much meat, which makes them unsuitable for meat production.

If you're planning on raising your Leghorns in the backyard, you might run into some problems with the neighbors. It is well known that Leghorns are noisy. They can also fly very well, which suggests that planning will be necessary to ensure they don't leave your yard.

Lastly, aggression might pose a challenge when it comes to Leghorn roosters. They are quite nervous and don't really enjoy human company. Whenever possible, they prefer being alone and not frequently disturbed. Overall, Leghorns are fantastic for egg production, and they're a good breed for a beginner to start with, as they're very hardy and don't get sick easily.

Rhode Island Red

No list of popular chicken breeds would be complete without the lovely Rhode Island Red. These chickens have been bred to produce meat and eggs but are mostly used for egg production. They produce large, brown eggs and are known for great-tasting eggs and meat.

There are two types of Rhode Island Reds—heritage Rhode Island Reds and industrial Rhode Island Reds. The industrial strain of this breed is a bit smaller and will most likely produce more eggs. They have been bred to flourish on commercial farms. They're great for production; however, the taste of their meat and eggs will be very similar to other large-scale poultry products.

It's always better to try and get heritage Rhode Island Reds. This breed is great for free-range farming, and they're considered very curious and intelligent. You'll notice that they are hardy, don't get sick often, and are also suited for cold and warm climates.

This breed is more likely to be broody than the Leghorn, but it also differs from flock to flock. In terms of temperament, the roosters can become quite aggressive, and they don't do well when kept among other breeds. They will most likely fight with- and injure smaller breeds.

I would definitely recommend this breed to any beginner or seasoned chicken farmer. They're an overall fantastic breed to raise and don't have many health challenges, which is always a massive advantage.

Black Australorp

This breed is easily one of my top three chicken breeds to raise. With their black feathers that have a greenish glimmer in the sunlight, they're nothing short of magnificent to look at! It's not just their great looks that make Australorps famous. These chickens are fantastic layers as well as meat producers, making them an ideal dual-purpose breed.

Their eggs are brown and can differ in size between medium and large. The Guinness World Record for laying the most eggs is actually held by a Black Australorp (Countryside Contributor, 2019). This might be an anomaly, but they still lay around 260 eggs per year on average, which is quite impressive.

If you're looking for a docile, friendly breed, this is the one! They enjoy interacting with humans and can form close bonds once they become accustomed to them. They're great with children and other animals and will even be playful at times.

The Australorp is better suited for colder climates, as their black feathers may cause heat exhaustion in hot climates. They can be kept in warmer climates if the necessary precautions are taken to prevent overheating, such as providing sufficient shelter and water.

If you intend on keeping this breed with other breeds, you should make sure that the other breeds are also relatively docile, or they might bully your Australorps. I always say that the Australorp is like a lovable, cuddly teddy bear that loves treats.

They're perfect for keeping on a homestead but will need space to move around, as they're prone to becoming overweight if they don't get enough exercise. Health wise, you won't have many problems with this breed, and they're also a great choice for a beginner.

HOUSING YOUR CHICKENS: COOPS, RUNS, AND FREE RANGING

Adequate housing is an extremely important part of raising chickens. It could mean the difference between success and failure of your project. Housing serves as a shelter to keep your chickens safe from predators, warm, dry, and comfortable.

Housing options are diverse, but it is crucial that your coop complies with the following rules regardless of what type you choose:

- Chickens should be protected from the elements, such as rain and storms.
- The coop should be well-ventilated, but ventilation holes should be small and strategically placed in order to prevent predators from entering the coop.

- The coop should be predator-proof.
- There shouldn't be a draft in the coop, as this can lead to your animals getting sick.
- The coop should be strong and sturdy.
- There should be no sharp edges or things that can injure the chickens.
- Your chickens should be protected against extreme weather conditions, whether it's heat or cold.

In addition to the chicken coop, your chickens will need an area outside where they can move around. This area is usually referred to as the *chicken run.* Once again, there are countless ways to set up a chicken run, and the chosen method will depend on your unique situation and needs.

There are two main ways to get housing for your chickens—building your own coop and run or buying them. The choice you make will depend on your budget, time available to spend on the project, available materials, space requirements, climate, and other environmental factors.

If you're planning on breeding with your flock or raising your chickens for eggs, your coop will need to have nesting boxes. These are areas where the hen will feel safe enough to lay her eggs and nest on them. You don't need one nesting box per hen, but I would recommend having at least one for every three hens.

A nesting box should be comfortable and packed with soft material to prevent damage to eggs and injury to hens. You will also need to place perches or roosting bars in the coop where the chickens can sleep at night. Each bird will need about 12 in. of roosting space and about 4 sq ft of general space in the coop (Toney, 2022).

The amount of space needed per bird will differ from breed to breed. Larger breeds will need more space, and smaller breeds will need less space. It's better to have extra space than to cram all your chickens into a coop that is way too small.

. . .

Building a Coop

Building a coop may seem like a massive task if you're not an experienced builder, but it doesn't have to be. The advantage is that you get to customize your coop and run exactly how you want them, and make them as big or small as you prefer. Creating your own design is always fun because you can create the perfect fit for your unique environment and situation.

An important thing to remember when building your coop and run is that you should always leave room for possible future expansion. If you design your coop in a way that will make future expansion hard to do, it will end up causing a headache further down the line.

If you live in an area where you encounter natural disasters frequently, such as tornadoes or big hail storms, this is a serious aspect to consider when deciding on where to place your coop. Try to keep it away from anything that may fall on it, such as large branches. Take sunlight into consideration as well, as keeping the right temperature in the coop is paramount.

Your coop should be made from durable materials that can withstand the climate. Wood is a favorite when it comes to chicken coops, and you'll find that it works very well. Your coop should be insulated well, especially in colder areas.

Ventilation is of utmost importance in your chicken coop, and you can place mesh windows near the roof. The mesh will keep predators and pests out while still providing sufficient ventilation. It's better to place any openings close to the roof, as this will make it harder for predators to try and enter through them.

Predators are a serious concern to all chicken farmers, so your coop should be able to shut securely in the evenings. When it comes to the chicken run, you should consider which predators pose the biggest problem in your area. If there is a problem with aerial predators, for instance, you will have to cover the top of the chicken run with chicken wire.

Even with the name *chicken wire,* this material is not suitable to enclose your entire chicken run. While it's good for keeping chickens in, it's not particularly sturdy and won't keep most predators out. The better option is to use galvanized square welded wire, otherwise known as hardware mesh. Get the smallest squares that you possibly can. This will not only prevent predators from getting in but also pests such as rodents.

Elevating the coop from the ground is always a good idea. This is just another preventative measure to keep predators out, with the added bonus that the wooden floor won't rot fast. In case you decide to elevate the coop, make sure it's high enough for a chicken to stand comfortably underneath. This will prevent things like rodents and snakes from nesting under the coop.

When building your coop and run, make sure that you reinforce them as much as possible. You can either build a portable coop and run or stationary ones. I prefer the portable option, as you can let your chickens *graze* on pasture and move them often in order to have them fertilize more soil at a time. You can also move the coop and run in times of heavy rain, floods, and mud.

The size of your project will have an impact on which option you choose. If you're planning a large project with hundreds or thousands of chickens, the portable option will probably be a bit more challenging. Your coop will most likely be stationary, as it will be too big to move around.

Free range, by definition, means "giving your chickens enough outside space for them to forage for insects and move around comfortably." If you choose to have a stationary coop, you can always have a portable chicken run. You can move the run around the coop every few days or so.

The great thing about building your own coop is that you can get as creative as you'd like. You can also make use of some recycled materials, and your self-built coop will be much cheaper than one you can buy if you play your cards right. Chances are that it will be better suited for your project due to the fact that you designed it yourself, and sturdier in the long run as well.

If you don't have experience in building, don't worry. Learning a new skill is always a plus, and while you may encounter some challenges, you'll be very proud of yourself once the project is finished! Family and friends can enjoy this activity with you, or you can do it alone to improve your skills.

If you want to have the experience of building your own coop but don't feel like you want to create your own design, consider buying a chicken coop kit. These kits will come with everything you need to build your coop with detailed instructions. I know that some may be tempted to throw out the instructions and figure it out themselves, but I would advise you not to do so. Follow the instructions carefully to ensure that your coop is structurally sound.

Buying a Coop

Buying a new coop and run can cost anywhere from $250 and upwards. If you have the budget, it's a great way to save some time, but not always the best option for your project. The chances that you will find a coop and run that perfectly fit your needs and space aren't zero but aren't very high either.

The great thing about buying a coop and run is that the work has already been done for you, and all you need to do is pop in your little friends and get started. Less work and effort are required to get everything set up, and you don't have to spend time on hard labor. This can be a good solution for someone who isn't quite confident enough to take on their own building project just yet.

Something to think about is that it will be challenging to customize a ready-bought coop and run to fit your situation better. You will also most likely not have many choices when it comes to the design. The other concern is the quality of the coop. If we're being honest, you get what you pay for in this area of the project. If you choose the cheaper options, the materials used to build the coop will most likely not be very durable.

You can consider buying a used coop, which is not a bad idea if you're ready to do some inevitable repairs. This can also save you some time and money. The other option is to get a professional to build a coop for you. This is probably the most expensive option, but this way, you get to choose what it looks like and what the quality of the materials will be.

In the end, it all comes down to what will fit your project better. Whether you buy or build, it's important to ensure that the coop lives up to the standards mentioned earlier. If it doesn't, your chickens won't be doing very well, and your project may fail. In the next chapter, we'll be looking at the basics of daily care for your animals, as well as things like health problems and solutions and behavior.

CHAPTER 2
FROM CHICK TO CHICKEN— PRACTICALITIES AND CARE

We can see a thousand miracles around us every day. What is more supernatural than an egg yolk turning into a chicken?
–S. Parkes Cadman

For most beginners, caring for their first flock can be very intimidating. You might look up a few tips online and feel somewhat overwhelmed by all the different information. Not only is there too much to work through, but a lot of it can be very conflicting as well. This is why I've made sure to include this chapter that will focus on the following three aspects of caring for your chickens:

- nutrition and feed
- healthcare
- handling and behavior

As a beginner, it can be difficult to try and focus on everything at once. Throughout this chapter, these three important factors will be explained in a way that makes following through on your project as easy as possible.

NUTRITION AND FEED: ENSURING YOUR CHICKENS ARE HAPPY AND HEALTHY

Chickens have a few main nutritional requirements:

- water
- proteins
- carbohydrates
- vitamins and minerals
- fat
- dietary fiber

Water

As any animal needs water to survive, chickens are very dependent on water for their health and survival. Water helps them digest food, regulate body temperature, yield a healthy production, and complete other normal daily bodily functions.

If your chickens aren't getting enough water, they also won't eat enough feed. Clean water should be available for your chickens at any given time. Mature hens will need about 17 oz of water each daily (Lesley, 2021).

There are a few different types of drinkers on the market, and each of them has their own pros and cons. The most important thing is that the drinker should be easy to clean, keep debris and droppings out as much as possible, and be accessible to the chickens.

A very popular and effective option for a drinker is the bucket drinker, also called the siphon drinker. It looks like a bucket turned upside down into a bowl. As the chickens drink the water from the bowl, it will be replenished with water from the bucket. These drinkers are usually made from hard plastic, meaning that it is durable. They are also quite easy to clean.

Some chicken farmers use regular bowls as drinkers. Although it is functional, it is definitely not ideal. As a result of the contamination that is so often found with this option, bowls must be refilled and cleaned more frequently.

Some commercial farmers use automatic drinkers, also known as nipple drinkers. These drinkers completely eliminate the chance of contamination, and you don't have to refill anything as they are usually connected to a water system. These drinkers are the easiest and probably the best option, as the height can also be adjusted to be accessible to your chickens regardless of their age and size.

For the backyard chicken farmer, I would say that bucket drinkers are the best option. The challenge with automatic drinkers is that the drinkers are a bit tricky to install and can be a bit more expensive, while bucket drinkers are inexpensive and easy to work with.

Protein

As we've discussed, the amount of protein in the diet of your animals is influenced by a few different things, especially the production stage, and age. Something else that will increase the need for protein in their diets is molting. Chickens will usually shed their feathers once a year to regrow new, healthy feathers.

During this time, they don't produce eggs and will need more protein than usual. When choosing feed for your chickens, look at the protein content of the feed. Ensure that the protein is sufficient for the specific life stage that your chickens are in.

According to *Minimum Protein Needs for Chickens* (n.d.), starter feed for broiler chicks will usually contain around 23% protein, and the finisher will contain around 10% protein, whereas, in layer chicks, the starter will contain around 20% protein, the grower feed will contain 14% protein, and the maintenance layer feed will contain 16% protein.

. . .

Carbohydrates

Carbohydrates are a major source of energy for chickens and are also usually the largest percentage of chicken feed. Carbohydrates come from different grains included in chicken diets, which include barley, sorghum, corn, and more.

Carbohydrates are divided into two categories—digestible and indigestible. Digestible carbohydrates like starch are used for energy, and non-digestible carbohydrates like cellulose are used to aid in digestion and intestinal health (Vest & Dale, 2022).

Vitamins and Minerals

Vitamins and minerals play many vital roles in the bodies of your chickens. Vitamin deficiencies aren't too common but can occur if you're not feeding your animals a balanced diet. These deficiencies may sometimes only present visible symptoms once already quite severe.

Your chickens will need sufficient amounts of vitamins in order to keep their immune systems healthy. Certain vitamins are needed to use minerals in the body, which means that a deficiency might lead to the animal being unable to utilize all the minerals they need.

As minerals and vitamins work in conjunction with one another in the body, it is important to keep a balance between them. Too much of a certain mineral or vitamin may cause an imbalance and more problems.

If you're worried that your chickens might encounter some vitamin or mineral deficiencies, you can give them a vitamin and mineral supplement, which is available online and at most poultry supply stores.

Feeding your chickens an array of vegetables and greens will certainly provide them with a lot of vitamins and minerals and will also be good for their digestive systems. However, if you're feeding your chickens a complete feed, anything else fed to them will dilute the amount of vitamins they get from it.

Fats

Apart from providing your chickens with energy, fat plays a key role in the absorption of fat-soluble vitamins. Having learned just how important vitamins are to our animals' diet, it's easier to understand why it is so essential to have enough fat in their diet, to be able to absorb them. Vitamins are not all fat-soluble, but the ones that are are quite important. *Fat-soluble vitamins* refer to "vitamins A, D, E, and K."

Furthermore, fat is a very tasty addition to the feed of your chickens. Not only will this addition make it taste better, but it will also reduce the amount of dustiness. Feed that is too powdery may cause respiratory issues in chickens when they breathe in the dust particles.

When chickens digest fats, they don't generate as much metabolic heat as they do when they digest other things, such as protein. Less fat in the diet means more heat in the body, which may lead to heat exhaustion in very warm temperatures. Fats should always be included in the diet to keep your animals healthy and happy. The least amount of fat to be included in the diets of layers is 5% (*Crude Fat in Layer Nutrition*, 2017).

Dietary Fiber

Dietary fiber aids in keeping the digestive system of the chicken healthy. It will help bulk up feed, move it along in the tract, and regulate the pace at which it does so. While certain fibers are digestible, insoluble or indigestible fibers are needed in the diet to ensure that no toxins build up in the digestive tract. Including adequate amounts of insoluble fiber in the diet has [been] shown to reduce cannibalism and feather plucking (Pietsch, 2022).

Grit

Chickens have been known to swallow fine rocks to aid in digestion and grinding of their food. Chickens don't have teeth, which often results in them swallowing pieces of food whole. The food is moved to the crop, where it stays until it is fine enough to move down to the stomach.

These fine rocks also move to the crop, where they help your chickens grind down large pieces of food into smaller, more digestible ones. This is where grit comes in. Grit is available in two forms, namely soluble and insoluble. In simpler terms, the first type is dissolved in water, whereas the second type is not.

Insoluble grit is made from granite or flint. This merely aids in digestion and has no other functions. Soluble grit is made from sea shells and can also provide your chickens with a good source of calcium. Chickens that don't ingest anything else but ready-bought feed generally don't need grit added to their diets; however, chickens that are left to forage or get kitchen scraps will need it to break down the larger pieces of food.

You can mix in the grit with the feed of the chickens, or you can place it separately for your chickens to help themselves. When adding it to their feed, only a very small amount is needed. This can be as little as 0.5% of the total amount of feed given (Boggs, 2014). I prefer having the grit separately, as chickens won't consume more than they need at any given stage.

FACTORS THAT INFLUENCE THE NUTRITIONAL REQUIREMENTS OF CHICKENS

The first factor that we'll be looking at is genetics. Each individual chicken may have slightly differing nutritional needs from the next due to their genetics. It is common for farmers to use selective breeding to breed chickens that require less feed and nutrients but produce a higher yield. Their offspring will receive the good genes. This has an impact on individual chickens, as well as the breed itself.

Different breeds will have wildly varying nutritional needs. We've looked at a few different breeds and their characteristics, and through this, we can clearly see that certain breeds have been bred to use less feed and nutrients than others. Some breeds, such as the Cornish Cross, will become extremely obese and unhealthy if fed the same amount of feed as other, slower-growing breeds.

Production levels have a great impact on the nutrients needed, and they vary from breed to breed, as well as strain to strain. Layer breeds will also have different nutritional needs than broiler breeds. Feed efficiency is the factor that we should be looking at here. You might think that higher production means a larger nutrient need, and in some cases, it does. However, as we once again saw by looking at the Cornish Cross as an example, some breeds will use feed more efficiently than others.

Moreover, the age of the chicken will make a difference in nutritional needs. The bigger your chickens grow, the more feed they will need. Composition is key, and all chicken feed is not the same. Between zero and six weeks, your chickens are growing rapidly and starting to get feathers. During this time, more protein is needed.

As the chickens grow, the protein content in their feed is usually lowered. As their growth slows down, they will need less protein.

Their protein requirements usually stabilize once they reach maturity.

When chickens are facing health issues, their nutrient requirements will also change. Depending on the health problem, they might need an increase in vitamins or protein and carbohydrates. As we appreciate chicken soup when we're not feeling well, they appreciate some extra nutrients to help them recover faster.

Layer hens in production will need more calcium and protein than their broiler counterparts. This is because they need enough nutrients to produce strong and healthy eggs and chicks in some cases. Higher egg production will mean a higher calcium need. In general, roosters will eat more than hens because they are also usually larger. Mating activity will increase the amount of energy needed and, therefore, also the nutrient requirements.

The amount of energy that chickens need is dependent on their activity level. If they are more active, they will need feed with higher energy content. If their space is confined and they don't move around very much, they will need less energy.

Chickens generally require feed with a higher energy level, and sometimes more feed in general, when temperatures are low. They release heat to the rest of the body through their metabolic processes, which means they consume more energy to regulate their body temperatures.

DIFFERENT TYPES OF CHICKEN FEED

As mentioned, chickens will have different nutritional needs depending on their age. There is chicken feed on the market, specially formulated for each age, containing all of the needed nutrients. This makes it much easier for the farmer, as they can simply feed the right feed at the right time, and they don't have to worry about formulating feed themselves.

There are organic and non-organic options on the market, of which I would definitely recommend organic. Non-organic feeds may contain chemicals and other harmful substances, which is why organic is a safer option if you want to move away from that. It is worth mentioning that organic feed will usually be more expensive but well worth it.

In the world of commercial farming, chicken feed producers have come up with a way to incorporate preventative medicine into certain feeds to help farmers combat health issues in the flock. Chicken farmers are faced with the choice between medicated and non-medicated chicken feed.

The medicated chicken feed contains amprolium, which is used to help prevent coccidiosis (Lehr, 2022). The only problem is that it's not guaranteed to work and may cause a thiamine deficiency in some cases. Thiamine, also known as vitamin B1, plays an essential role in chicken growth and development. A medicated feed shouldn't be given to chicks that have been vaccinated since it might affect the vaccine.

Unmedicated feed is the more natural approach, and I definitely prefer it over medicated feed. It's all about letting your animals build their own immunity and providing them with an environment that limits the chances of infections. When allowing your chickens to build their own immunity, they're becoming stronger and more resilient in the long run. Ultimately, it is up to each individual to make their own decision on which option they want to go with.

The first feed your chickens will be introduced to is starter feed. As I've mentioned, this has a higher protein content because the chickens will be growing rapidly during this stage. The yolk of the egg provides the chicks with all the moisture and nutrients they need in the first 24 hours of their lives, which means that they don't need additional feed and water during this time. The starter feed is usually fed from the day after your chicks hatch until they're 8 weeks old.

Layers

As chicks grow into pullets, which is between the ages of 8 and 16 weeks, their nutritional needs will change, and so will their feed. They are then introduced to grower feed. This is fed to them for the entire pullet stage. The protein content will be slightly lower than the starter feed, as they're not growing as fast anymore.

After the pullet stage, chickens are considered to be mature. This is any age from 16 weeks and up. From there, you will feed your chickens a maintenance layer feed, depending on their production.

Broilers

Depending on the breed you're raising, broilers can be ready to slaughter between 8 and 12 weeks (*About chickens farmed for meat,* n.d.). Some breeds may even be ready to slaughter by week 6. Ensure that you've done sufficient research on the breed you're raising and when they should be slaughtered.

Because broilers are slaughtered at such a young age, they will be fed a starter until week four, after which they will be fed a finisher, which will help them gain the right amount of muscle for slaughter.

HEALTHCARE ESSENTIALS: PROTECTING YOUR FLOCK FROM DISEASES AND PREDATORS

One of the most intimidating parts of starting out with your first flock is keeping it healthy. I remember panicking every time a chicken just looked like there might be something slightly wrong when I first started out.

In this area of raising chickens, there is no such thing as too much research. However, when doing research, ensure that you're doing so from reputable sources. In my experience, the best research that you could possibly do would be to ask chicken farmers in your area about the health problems they're facing with their flocks.

Search engines can be very helpful, but you might find yourself drowning in confusing and conflicting information. Nothing beats personal experience, and you will learn so much more spending an afternoon with a seasoned chicken farmer than you will on the internet.

In this section, we'll be going over some of the most common health issues you might encounter with your flock, how to prevent them, and how to treat them. The basic tools and information you need to keep your animals healthy can be found here.

UNDERSTANDING COMMON HEALTH ISSUES AND FIRST AID FOR CHICKENS

Once you start having conversations with other chicken farmers from all over, you'll notice that common health problems in flocks differ from area to area. This is due to an array of factors, including climate, feed, living conditions, and other fauna commonly found in the area.

Parasites

The first health issue that we'll be looking at is parasites. Parasites are categorized into two sections—endo- and ectoparasites. Taking nutrients or anything else from another organism for their own gain at the expense of the host, makes an organism a parasite.

Endoparasites are organisms that will infect your chickens internally. Your first thought may be *worms,* and you're absolutely right.

A common endoparasite in chickens is worms, particularly round-worms and tapeworms.

The unfortunate truth is that all animals will have worms at some stage in their lives, and most chickens will have a few worms in their systems. It usually won't bother them too much until they are infested and the number of worms they have is no longer within an acceptable range. This is also when they will start showing signs such as an abnormal stool, visible worms in droppings, or weight loss and weakness.

Chickens will get worms from eating insects or contaminated droppings. Free-range chickens will certainly eat some contaminated insects at some stage, which means infection is almost inevitable. Like I said, most chickens will have some worms, and it's completely normal. However, once you start seeing the signs, it's no longer normal.

Different worms will require different treatments, and it's best to consult your local poultry vet about which products to use. In many cases, you also won't be able to get certain deworming medication over the counter, and you will need to see a vet anyway.

I always say that *poo patrol* is an integral part of chicken farming, and even though it might not be very pleasant, it can tell you a lot about the health of your chickens. Foamy droppings are one of the signs to look for if you're concerned about worms, but you may also see some worms in the droppings.

Protozoa are also considered "endoparasites and are small, single-celled organisms that can infect your chickens." The most common protozoa that infect chickens are called *coccidia*. Prolonged out-of-control infection with coccidia will lead to *coccidiosis*, which is harmful to chickens.

There are a few things that you can do to prevent coccidiosis. The first and probably easiest way to prevent infection is by regularly cleaning the coop and chicken run and keeping their bedding dry. Your chickens can become infected by ingesting the eggs of the parasite, which are found in the droppings of infected chickens. If you ensure that your chickens have minimal contact with droppings, you can also reduce the chances of them becoming infected.

You also have the option to buy vaccinated chicks at the hatchery. Always enquire about vaccinations when buying new chicks, whether you buy them from hatcheries or local farmers. You don't have to buy vaccinated animals, and whether you choose to do so or not is entirely up to you.

Depending on where you live, your flock may have different types of ectoparasites, like lice, mites, and fleas. Your flock may get these parasites from wild birds and other animals in the area, and minimizing contact with wild animals will also reduce the chances of infestation.

An infestation of ectoparasites can have an impact on the production and fertility of your animals and may have other symptoms, such as skin irritation and scaly legs. Something to keep in mind about ectoparasites is that they often lay their eggs in surrounding areas as well as inside the coop and in the bedding.

This means that when you treat your chickens with a safe insecticide, you will have to treat the entire area that they use. This can include removing all of the bedding, treating every crack and corner of your coop, and placing new bedding in there.

You should always read all instructions on the container carefully before applying insecticides to your chickens. Ensure that you're using the right safety precautions for yourself as well. There are organic options on the market, and if your chickens show signs of scaly legs, you can merely apply petroleum jelly to suffocate the parasites.

· · ·

Wounds

As we get closer to the behavior section of this chapter, we'll be discussing wounds inflicted by other members of the flock. You will most likely see them quite clearly, as they may bleed or be in a bald spot.

Unfortunately, when chickens see a wound or bleeding on another chicken, they will start pecking at it. This is bad because it may increase the severity of the wound and cause infection. Upon seeing a wound on one of your chickens, depending on how serious it is, you may want to remove the injured chicken from the flock until they have healed.

There will be times when you might find that one specific chicken is a serial offender and constantly acts aggressively or injures other chickens. Removing them from the flock for a while until all of the chickens are healed and have no more wounds is a good idea.

You can apply a topical antibiotic wound spray or ointment to the wound and keep an eye on it. That's usually all that is necessary, but if the wound doesn't start healing after a few days, you should consult a vet. If the wound is on the feet of the chicken, you can use an antiseptic wound wash and bandage it up to reduce the chances of further injury (Lesley, 2022).

Viruses

Viruses can cause an array of problems in your flock, and the biggest issue is that they are incurable with antibiotics. One of the most significant viruses for you to be aware of is *bird flu*, also referred to as *avian influenza*.

There is no treatment for this virus, and if even one of your chickens is found to have contracted it, the entire flock will have to be culled. This is because the virus is highly contagious between chickens and may also infect humans. Although the chances of humans contracting the virus are significantly lower than other chickens, one can't be too careful.

Bird flu is mainly spread by waterfowl, which includes ducks, geese, and other wild birds that spend a lot of time around water. If there is a water source for these birds to gather close to where you keep your chickens, limiting contact between the wild birds and your chickens is essential.

Signs of infection include lethargy, low production, irregular droppings, sudden death, combs that may present purple, head swelling, no appetite, reduced water intake, discharge from nostrils —eyes and beaks—and coughing. You probably won't have all of these signs at once, but if you suspect your chickens may be infected, you should contact your local vet immediately.

The only way that we can really reduce the chances of infection with this disease is by practicing good biosecurity. This means that we should be mindful of transmittable diseases at all times and keep their area clean. If you or anyone else has been in contact with other birds or chickens, it's best to avoid contact with your chickens until you've changed your clothes and sterilized your hands.

When you visit areas with sources of water where waterfowl are present, you should avoid coming near your flock with the same clothes. Don't use other people's equipment unless it has been meticulously sterilized, and ensure that you're aware if a visitor has had contact with other flocks of birds recently before allowing them near your animals.

Another virus that is quite prevalent in chickens is *Newcastle disease.* This virus is not spread to humans but can cause your chickens to become very ill. You may see similar signs to bird flu with the addition of possible convulsions or tremors, as well as green diarrhea.

Similar to bird flu, our way of combating this virus lies in good biosecurity. There are also options for vaccinations against the virus on the market, but there is no guarantee that they won't still contract the virus. Their symptoms might appear less severe if vaccinated, but you will still need to implement good biosecurity.

Other viruses that may cause problems in your flock include Marek's disease, infectious bronchitis, and pox (Morishita, 1996). There are vaccinations for Marek's disease on the market, but once again, there is still no guarantee.

If you suspect at all that your flock is infected by a virus, you should contact your local vet or authorities as soon as possible. It's important for them to know what's going on in order to keep other poultry flocks in the area safe. They will also be able to advise you on the steps to take next.

Bacterial Infections

Bacterial infections can range from mild to dangerous in the chicken flock but can be treated with antibiotics. *Fowl cholera* is a common bacterial disease caused by bacteria that can be spread to your flock by other wild animals.

Some animals can be carriers of the bacteria and won't show any symptoms. If this disease is a problem in your area, you can consider vaccinating your chickens against it. Contaminated clothing and equipment can also cause infection, which shows, once again, why we should be careful when using equipment from other poultry farms.

You may see a swollen face and feet as well as reduced production, fever, or sudden death. Even after you've successfully diagnosed and treated your chicken with this condition, they can remain carriers.

Another bacterial disease to be aware of is *bumblefoot*. This can be caused by a few things, including obesity, foot trauma and injury, and restricted blood flow to the feet. The bacteria will take their chance and infect the foot, causing swelling and pain. Even though the secondary bacterial infection can be treated with antibiotics, the initial problem should also be solved. Keeping an eye on the health of your chicken's feet and quickly treating wounds will help prevent this condition.

Mycoplasmosis, otherwise known as *Chronic Respiratory Disease,* is a bacterial infection that infects the sinuses and respiratory systems of chickens. You may observe some discharge from the nasal and eyes as well as coughing. There are vaccinations available for this condition but will not prevent it completely if your biosecurity isn't up to standard.

Overall, most bacterial infections can be successfully treated by antibiotics, but in some cases, the chickens affected may remain carriers. In those cases, depending on the severity of the infection, culling the affected chickens may be a better option. Good biosecurity and sourcing your animals from dependable, infection-free sources is impeccable.

WHEN TO CONSULT A VET

Having a vet near you is very necessary when it comes to the health of your animals. If you're ever unsure of a certain health condition in your flock, rather be safe than sorry and consult your local vet. Vets will be able to help you with a diagnosis and treatment and offer you some information about how you can prevent something in the future.

When it comes to reporting illness to the local vet or authorities, you should never play the guessing game. If you have sudden unexplained death or respiratory issues in your flock, the safe bet is to notify them immediately. It can either be a false alarm, and you can get the right treatment and advice for your flock, or it can be a serious issue such as bird flu, where you run the risk of infecting other flocks in the area.

. . .

STRATEGIES FOR PREDATOR-PROOFING YOUR CHICKEN COOP

No matter where you go, there will always be predators of some kind around. Predators can be a big concern and annoyance when it comes to raising chickens. There are a few different predators that you should be aware of, and predator-proofing your coop will save you a lot of frustration.

The types of predators you'll encounter will differ from area to area, and having some general knowledge on how to keep your flock safe from a variety of them will be very helpful, no matter which predators you face. Hence, it is essential to find out which predators are most prevalent in your area. This will help you prepare to face them better.

The first and most important thing that you can do to keep your flock safe from predators is to lock them inside their coop at night. This will ensure that any nocturnal predators such as owls, skunks, or raccoons can't get to them. Your coop should be able to lock up tightly while still having some ventilation holes. These holes should preferably be covered by very fine and strong squared wire mesh, which will prevent snakes and rats from gaining access to the coop.

Your coop should be made from strong and durable material that can't be breached by predators. Do regular maintenance to ensure that any rotten wood is replaced before it becomes an access point for predators. The coop should be strong enough to withstand the elements as well as an attack from a predator.

Remove any nearby debris, tall grass, and other plants that may serve as a hiding place for predators from the area of the coop. If there is anything such as food scraps or fallen fruits, which might attract wildlife and predators, be sure to remove them often. The less you attract them, the less they will be a problem.

Aerial predators such as hawks and owls can be kept away by covering the chicken run with squared wire mesh or a fine net at the top. When it comes to the sides of the run, using strong squared wiring is highly recommended. Smaller squares are always better, as they will keep smaller predators out as well.

Some predators have the habit of digging underneath the wire. This can be prevented by ensuring that the mesh sides are at least 1 ft deep into the soil on all sides (Ask UNH Extension, 2019). It can be costly to use good-quality mesh or other predator-proof parts for your chicken run and coop, but at the end of the day, it will be worth it. Protecting your animals should always be the priority.

HANDLING AND BEHAVIOR: BUILDING A POSITIVE RELATIONSHIP WITH YOUR CHICKENS

The Pecking Order

Though some might think chickens are simple creatures, the truth is that they are quite sophisticated and serious when it comes to the hierarchy in the flock. The hierarchy in a chicken flock is often referred to as the *pecking order.*

Chickens take the pecking order very seriously, and each member of the flock has a specific place in this order. The hierarchy is established when the chickens challenge each other, so you can expect some scuffles from time to time.

Stronger, more dominant chickens will be at the top of the pecking order, and the older and weaker birds will be lower in ranking. The flock will start establishing who goes where in the pecking order at around week one, and by week six, the pecking order is stable.

Every time a new chicken is added to the flock or when a chicken is removed and isolated because of sickness or injury, the pecking order changes. When a chicken who has been isolated for some time is then reintroduced back into the flock, there will be a few scuffles to reestablish the pecking order.

The chickens at the top play the role of protectors, as they are the strongest and the fastest. They are also entitled to the best of everything, including food, nesting spots, and roosting spots. Fights among chickens for their place in the pecking order may become violent at times, but it's important to let them scuffle it out up to a certain point.

You should separate them if they sustain serious injuries. Note that once you reintroduce them, they will most likely fight again. The top chicken will usually be a rooster, but in flocks that have no roosters, a hen will be appointed the top role.

Learning

Chickens are very intelligent animals. They learn a lot from observing other chickens as well as humans. They enjoy playing and will often show very inquisitive behavior. They will play with toys when provided to them, and also enjoy playing with each other occasionally. Things like mirrors or snacks hanging from a string will definitely catch their attention.

Newly hatched chicks don't know how to eat or drink and are usually taught to do so by their mothers. If you're hatching eggs yourself, you will need to take on that role and teach them. You can do so by placing their beaks inside the food and water containers. Thereafter, they will start eating and drinking. It may take a few tries, but it is relatively easy to do.

HOW TO SOCIALIZE WITH CHICKENS

Chickens are very vocal animals. They mainly communicate through sounds and body language. It might sound unusual, but talking to your chickens while you tend to them will help them get to know you better. They will start to recognize your voice above others, and speaking to them in a gentle tone will encourage interaction with you.

If you're raising chickens from eggs, chances are that they will be quite docile and comfortable around you. However, if you're raising chickens from an older age, and you got them from somewhere else, they might be a little bit jumpy around you or afraid.

The key to creating a bond between you and chickens that are afraid of humans is to spend as much time with them as possible. Allow them to get used to you and your movements. They will observe you intently, so speaking to them and gently moving around will let them feel a little bit more at ease. Never make any sudden or intimidating movements around your flock.

You might not even realize it, but you are also part of the pecking order by default. Most of the time, you will be seen as the top of the hierarchy. Therefore, they will look to you for food and protection. In flocks where the chickens don't socialize with humans, they might see you as a threat in the beginning. As they start warming up to you, you'll become a part of the pecking order.

Food is a great motivator to get your chickens to interact with you. Snacks such as mealworms, carrots, cucumber, and lettuce are usually a great hit in the flock, and it will have your chickens loving you in no time. At first, they might be a little too nervous to hold, but once they start trusting you, you can start trying to pick them up.

When attempting to hold your chickens, always be extremely gentle, and don't hold them too tight. Your chicken shouldn't feel like it's fighting for its life. Some chickens just don't like being held, and having a good bond with them means respecting that boundary as well. Other chickens may be shy or scared at first, but will eventually enjoy being held very much and might even jump on your lap themselves once they're comfortable.

DEALING WITH AGGRESSIVE BIRDS

A problem with being a part of the pecking order is that you will be challenged for the top position every once in a while. Hens won't usually challenge humans, but some roosters may be very aggressive and willing to challenge you.

This can become dangerous, as roosters can really pack a punch with those claws and that beak. This is also a problem if you have other pets or children. Just like with the pecking order within the flock, in the rooster's mind, the winner will take the top position and have authority over the rest of the flock.

This means if you back down or run away, the rooster may continuously try to dominate you and become a menace. Once you turn your back on the aggressive bird, you're telling it that it has authority over you, which is the worst thing you can do.

While ensuring that you're wearing clothes that will reduce the chance of injury or even protective gear, you should stand tall and face the rooster. Having something like a broom or a bucket is very helpful, as this can be used to keep the rooster from jumping on you.

Try not to injure the rooster, but make sure it doesn't injure you. Show your dominance by making yourself look big and making noise. This may not work the first time, but if you keep doing this until the rooster backs down, you're guaranteed a top spot.

If you have a chicken that is particularly aggressive toward your other birds and you, you can remove them from the flock and keep them in a separate enclosure. If you keep them separate in a way that they can still look at the other chickens, they may learn to behave differently. Be aware that once they are relocated back into the flock, there will be some scuffles.

Very aggressive behavior may be a genetic trait, and if a chicken just refuses to become less aggressive, it's not a good idea to try and breed with these birds. Removing them from the flock entirely may be the only option you have at the end of the day if you've tried everything.

CHAPTER 3
THE REWARDS OF RAISING CHICKENS

Hard work pays off if you're patient enough to see it through.
–Michael Chandler

While some people start raising chickens because they love animals or enjoy watching them, the majority of us do it for the rewards that can be reaped from it. Even though being around your animals and observing nature work in its majesty are some of the most soul-fulfilling experiences, these are usually considered a bonus next to meat and eggs.

THE GIFT OF EGGS: FROM COLLECTION TO KITCHEN

Eggs are considered a superfood due to the high quality of protein they contain. Let's be honest. Eggs go with almost anything! If you enjoy supermarket eggs, get ready to have your mind blown. You'll notice that organic eggs have a much brighter and more orange color than supermarket eggs.

This can be attributed to the healthier lifestyle of chickens being fed organic foods. Organic eggs contain much higher levels of vitamins and other essential nutrients. Overall, they have a rich taste, and you won't be able to get enough of them once you've had them.

Different breeds will lay differently sized and colored eggs, and a handy trick to know what color eggs your hens will lay is to look at their little ear holes. If it is red, your hen will lay brown eggs, whereas white ear holes indicate that they will lay white eggs.

The breed that you choose when it comes to the color of the eggs is entirely up to personal preference, as there isn't really a difference in nutrients and taste. The amount of eggs you get from your hens will also depend on the breed, as discussed, but you can expect one egg per hen roughly every one to two days.

BEST PRACTICES FOR EGG COLLECTION AND STORAGE

The breed you've chosen will have an impact on the amount of broodiness of your hens. If you're raising chickens solely for the purpose of collecting eggs, broodiness isn't always a good trait. If your hens are broody, you might have a little bit of a hard time collecting their eggs.

It's crucial that you check for new eggs in the nesting boxes every morning, as well as somewhere in the late afternoon. The longer you leave eggs in the coop, the bigger the chances are of them getting damaged. Your nesting boxes should be lined with a soft material to prevent breakage or cracks of eggs. Straw or coop bedding are both good options. Ensure that the nesting boxes are set up in such a way that the eggs won't be able to roll out easily.

Always be gentle when approaching the coop to collect eggs. You can lure the hens from the nesting boxes with treats and food and collect the eggs when they get up. This will cause less disturbance than having to chase the hen out of the nesting box. You might find that a broody hen can be reluctant to get off of her eggs, and you may have to take the eggs out from under it. This is not ideal, and you might get some resistance in the form of an angry hen. I've always found that luring them off with food works best.

There are many products on the market designed specifically for collecting eggs, and you will probably find such a product easily on Amazon or at stores such as Walmart. However, in my opinion, any sturdy container lined with something soft enough to protect the eggs from damage will work just fine. Be mindful of eggs bumping into each other in the container, as this may cause them to crack.

If you find broken or cracked eggs in the coop, you should clean it up immediately. By doing so, chickens will be prevented from eating the eggs and learning how to crack them for themselves.

When it comes to storing your organic fresh eggs, cardboard egg cartons are the most cost-effective option. The market offers a wide selection of egg storage options, from plastic to glass and even ceramic. The container you choose for storage is entirely up to you, but make sure it is sturdy enough to keep your eggs safe.

CLEANING YOUR EGGS

Eggs are naturally covered by a wax layer for protection called the cuticle. This is designed to keep bacteria from entering the egg as the embryo grows. When collecting your eggs, it's best to get rid of eggs covered in droppings. Moreover, you should avoid washing eggs with soap at all costs. The reason for this is that washing the egg can remove its cuticle and contaminate it with bacteria. In the absence of the cuticle, bacteria can easily pass through the pores of eggshells.

If the eggs are a little bit dirty, you can use a soft cloth to gently wipe them down or a very fine grit sandpaper to remove any marks. You may use a little bit of water, but only if absolutely necessary. Be careful not to damage the eggs in the process. Also, ensure that you change the bedding in the nesting boxes often to avoid getting the eggs dirty.

I would recommend refrigerating your organic eggs, as this will make them last longer. You can keep them in the refrigerator for five to six weeks (Maclean, n.d.). If you choose to keep your eggs at room temperature, you will have to use them within two weeks.

DELICIOUS, HEALTHY RECIPES FEATURING FRESH EGGS

The first thing you'll want to do after collecting your first batch of fresh, organic, and delicious eggs is to try them! In this section, I'll be giving you a few basic healthy recipes that you can use to incorporate your harvest into your daily routine.

Garlic and Cheese Omelet

What better way to start out than making a tasty omelet? An omelet is an easy and healthy meal to prepare. The beauty of the omelet is that you can put anything on it that you like. From bacon to tomatoes, to mince, to plain cheese; it all just works! For this recipe, you can use any type of cheese that you prefer; however, cheddar works best.

Prep time: 2 minutes.

Cook time: 10 minutes.

Ingredients: 2 eggs, 1 tbsp olive oil, 10 g cheese, salt, pepper, and garlic.

Directions:

1. Use a mixing bowl to mix together the eggs, garlic, salt, and pepper. You can also use any other seasoning that you like.
2. Place a non-stick pan on the stove on medium to low heat and wait for it to warm up a little bit.
3. Add the olive oil to the pan and wait 20 seconds.
4. Pour the egg mixture into the pan and cover with a lid. Be sure to check on the omelet every minute or so.
5. Grate some cheese and pour it over the omelet once the egg is almost completely cooked.
6. Carefully remove the omelet from the pan and place it on a plate. You can now add any additional fillings or toppings to the omelet. Once your toppings are added, you can fold the omelet in half and serve.

———————

Roasted Egg and Chips

Who doesn't love potato chips? This recipe combines the healthiness of vegetables and eggs with the taste of an everyday all-time favorite. Besides being easy to make, this is also a fast breakfast or lunch option.

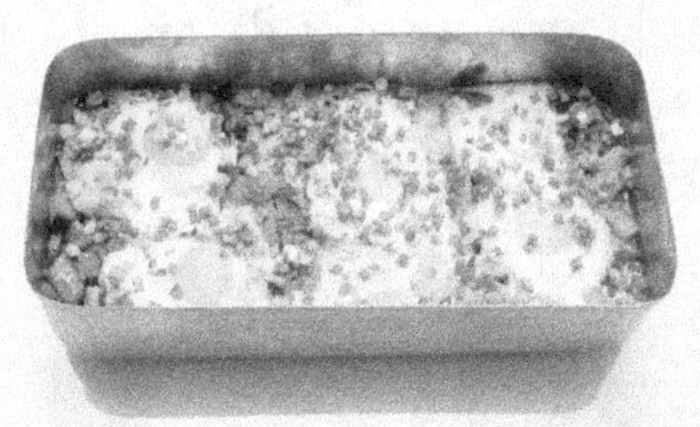

Serving size: 4.

Prep time: 10 minutes.

Cook time: 1 hour.

Ingredients: 2 tsp dried oregano, 2 tbsp olive oil, 4 eggs, mushrooms to taste, salt and pepper to taste, 2 onions, 500 g sliced potatoes.

Directions:

1. Preheat your oven to around 350°F.
2. Slice the onions into rounds.
3. Place the onions and potatoes in a non-stick oven pan and place in the oven.
4. Dribble the olive oil over the vegetables, and add salt and pepper to taste. Sprinkle the oregano over the contents of the pan.
5. Use a spatula and mix until all ingredients are covered in the olive oil. Place the pan in the oven and bake for 40–45 minutes.
6. Take the pan out of the oven carefully, place your mushrooms on top of the content of the pan, and bake for an additional 10 minutes.

7. Once your mushrooms are cooked, you can take out the pan again. Make four holes in between the vegetables and break an egg into each of the holes.
8. Place the pan back in the oven until the eggs are cooked, and serve.

Broccoli-Cheese Cup Eggs

Life can get busy sometimes, but breakfast is still the most important meal of the day. Whether you're in a hurry or not, this recipe will provide you with all the nutrients you need to get your day started.

Prep time: 5 minutes.

Cook time: 5 minutes.

Ingredients: 2 eggs, salt and pepper to taste, ¼ chopped bell pepper, 1 cup chopped broccoli, 2 tbsp milk, cooking spray, 1 chopped scallion, ½ cup grated cheese, and 1 tbsp water.

Directions:

1. Coat a large mug with cooking spray.
2. Microwave a cup with the broccoli and water on high until the broccoli is cooked.
3. Add the milk, eggs, salt and pepper, bell pepper, and scallion, and mix everything together with a fork.
4. Microwave the cup for 45 seconds and stir the content thoroughly. Place the cup back in the microwave and leave until the egg is cooked.
5. Add the cheese to the mug and place foil or a plate on top of the mug. Once the cheese is melted, you can enjoy your meal in a mug!

HOME-PROCESSED POULTRY: ETHICAL AND PRACTICAL ASPECTS

Many prospective backyard chicken farmers are very intimidated by the idea of processing their chickens for meat. This is very understandable, as it can be hard for someone with little to no experience to handle such an operation. In this section, we'll be going over everything you need to know about processing your chickens for meat ethically, as well as a few other helpful tips and tricks.

The Legal Aspect

Before considering processing chickens for meat in your backyard operation, it's important to look at the legal side of things. The laws on keeping poultry in your backyard can vary from country to country, state to state, area to area, and even neighborhood to neighborhood.

Certain laws will allow you to raise chickens in your backyard under certain regulations, but you won't be allowed to process them on-site. This means that you will have to find an establishment that can process your chickens for you.

Before considering raising chickens for meat, make sure you know the laws in your specific area. Speak to other local chicken farmers as well as the authorities, and ask for assistance if you don't understand any of the laws. It's better to make sure that you're in the right than to take a chance.

Slaughter Age and Weight

The first thing you should be sure of before slaughtering your chickens is the correct age and weight at which the specific breed needs to be slaughtered. As we've discussed, certain broiler breeds need to be slaughtered before a specific age, or they will become very unhealthy.

Ensure that you do sufficient research on the topic and document the age and weight of your chickens well in order to be sure of when to slaughter them. Depending on the breed you raise, your chickens will most likely be ready for slaughter between 8 and 10 weeks.

Some broiler breeds don't have a problem with *overgrowth* when they go past the normal slaughtering age. In these cases, you can wait longer to slaughter your chickens, but their meat might become less tender with age. However, older chicken's meat may be used for soups or stews. Once again, it all depends on the breed you choose. Also, remember that pullets will generally also weigh a lot less than cockerels.

I'm including this helpful table with some common slaughtering ages and weights for a few popular breeds. You don't have to go exactly by the book with these, and the ages and weights you choose to slaughter your chickens will depend on your unique circumstances. You can use this table as a general guideline:

. . .

BREED	SLAUGHTERING AGE	SLAUGHTERING WEIGHT
Cornish Cross	8–9 weeks	8–10 lbs
Big Red Broiler	12–14 weeks	5–7 lbs—depending on feed, they can weigh up to 10 lbs by slaughter age
Orpington	20–22 weeks	8–10 lbs
Dorking	19 weeks	7–9 lbs
Jersey Giant	16–21 weeks	11–13 lbs
Kosher King	11–12 weeks	5–7 lbs
Bresse	16–20 weeks	5–7 lbs
Croad Langshan	16–18 weeks	7–9 lbs

Before You Get Started

Before processing your chickens, you will need to take away their feed for at least a day. This will help prevent contaminating your meat cuts. Ensure that your workspace and tools are sanitized before starting. Dirty equipment can contaminate your meat, which is not a good thing. You can place your equipment in hot or boiling water and further clean them with an alkaline solution.

The hot water will ensure that all of the harmful bacteria are eliminated, and the alkaline solution will further ensure the cleanliness of your equipment. The surface that you use for processing should be easy to clean, such as a stainless steel surface. I find it easier to process chickens outside, as less cleanup is needed.

You will need the following equipment for processing your chickens:

- two very sharp knives
- a nearby water source to easily clean your equipment and working surface
- an alkaline solution or disinfectant
- a restrictive cone
- ice
- a cooler or tote in which ice can be placed
- protective clothing
- a few buckets
- a large stockpot or turkey fryer
- propane burner
- thermometer
- freezer bags or food sealer

A nearby water source will make it so much easier to clean up and get everything ready for processing your chickens. While processing, you will need water to keep your surfaces wet at all times. This makes it much easier to clean when the time comes and also keeps things clean as you go.

Furthermore, it's good to keep your disinfectant on hand even after you've sanitized everything, just in case. Always make sure to keep a cooler with ice ready to place chickens inside immediately after they've been processed. You don't want to wait until you have finished with all of the chickens until you keep them cool. It's never a good thing to leave them out in the heat.

Consider how many chickens you plan on processing, and plan out your freezer space accordingly. This is where the cooler with ice plays a very significant role. If you're processing many chickens, you might need something bigger, such as a trash can—clean, of course—or a tote bin.

If you don't place your processed chickens in ice water for enough time to allow them to cool down, you'll have a problem on your hands. Warmer birds take much longer to freeze in the freezer, and placing them inside the freezer while warm will result in the freezer thawing and your chickens going to waste.

By cooling your chickens down significantly before packaging and storage, you ensure that they freeze fast enough and don't start decomposing. Placing more ice on top of the chickens in the freezer is also a great way to speed up the process. Ensure that you have your packaging ready and you're using the correct packaging for your birds.

There are many options on the market when it comes to packaging, and vacuum-sealing your chickens is probably the best one if you have the equipment to do so. Always make sure the bags you use are specifically suited to be placed in the freezer.

The option that I use most often is poultry shrink bags. These bags are made specifically to store poultry. Once the bird has been fully processed, you can place it in a shrink bag. Thereafter, the shrink bag containing the bird is placed in a warm water bath. The bag will tighten around the bird, and by squeezing out all of the air and tying the top with a cable tie, you can safely store your produce.

Normal freezer bags can also be used to store your chickens; however, the presentation isn't as good as with shrink bags. If done properly, your produce can be stored in shrink bags for up to a year, whereas storing it in a freezer bag will give you around two months. Freezer bags also put your chickens at risk of freezer burn.

You want all of these little things to be in place before you start on slaughtering day. Processing should be a fast and specific thing, and scrambling around for equipment on processing day will slow things down significantly.

Ensure that you have a plan to get the processed, cooled-down chickens to their storage place quickly and efficiently. The idea is to get them in the freezer as fast as possible. This won't be a big concern if you're only processing a few chickens, but if you're processing many, you may want to consider getting a trailer or securing your transport.

Dispatching

To all beginners, I should warn that the first time you *dispatch* a chicken can be very uncomfortable. This is why we try to do it as fast and humanely as possible. You might have heard the saying, "Running around like a headless chicken" before. When the chicken is dispatched, we get what we call a *reflex action*. This refers to the nerve endings being triggered by a cut and sending down the message to the rest of the body to move. You should be prepared for a lot of movement and jerking once the job is done. This is completely normal and may scare beginners at first. This does not mean that the chicken is still alive but merely that the nerves have been triggered.

A *restrictive cone* is "a cone used to restrict the chicken for dispatching. It looks similar to a traffic cone and can be attached to a sturdy vertical surface, such as a wall or a tree." The small opening is positioned toward the floor. The chicken is picked up by its feet and carefully placed inside the restrictive cone head down.

The head is gently extended out of the small opening. The chicken will be restricted in the cone so as not to bruise any muscle or move around too much when preparing to dispatch. Ensure that you have a bucket or anything similar beneath the cone to collect any blood.

Once the chicken is placed inside the restrictive cone, place your hand on their head and gently extend it to expose the neck area. Dispatching can be done by cutting the jugular vein of the chicken. This is located near the beak on the side of the neck. Ensure that you don't cut the trachea, which runs down the middle of the neck under the beak. To do so effectively, part the feathers around the neck in order to expose as much skin as possible.

Don't try to cut through the feathers, as this will make your blade blunt, and you'll have a hard time getting to the neck quickly. Remember that we, as chicken farmers, should always have great respect for our animals, so doing this fast and painlessly is the goal.

Once you've exposed the skin of the neck under the beak, you can cut the jugular vein. There will be an immediate stream of blood from the neck, and the reflex action may kick in. You can now leave the chicken in the cone for around three minutes to ensure that all of the blood is drained from the carcass. Ensure that the bird is dispatched effectively before continuing with the process.

Defeathering

The next step is defeathering the chicken. This can be done by hand or by an electrical defeathering machine. You will need your large stockpot or turkey fryer, thermometer, and propane burner for this step. Fill the pot with water and heat it up until it is around 138–140°F, and place the chicken inside the pot for 30–75 seconds (Berry & Lester, n.d.). The time that it takes to soften the feathers enough for plucking may vary.

This process is called scalding. The carcass is placed in hot water to soften feathers enough so that they can easily be removed. This step is very important, and the water in your stock pot should under no circumstance be any warmer than the above temperature. This will result in cooking the bird. When you can feel that the feathers are easy to remove, you can remove the chicken from the pot. Be sure to feel the feathers on the legs and not the wings, as this will give you a better indication. It's a good idea to put a grate at the bottom of the pot to prevent the chicken from burning.

Once you've carefully removed the bird from the scalding pot, you will either use an electric automatic plucker or pluck the feathers by hand. If you're doing it by hand, you can place the bird on a flat surface and start removing the feathers section by section. Try to move as fast as possible to prevent the bird from cooling down too much and becoming hard to pluck. Having the bird under running water while doing so will make the process easier. You can collect all of the feathers and save them for composting.

Processing

Once all of the feathers have been removed, be sure to thoroughly rinse off any left-over feathers from the bird. This is the part where we physically process the chicken and get it ready for packaging and storage. It may seem that there is only one way to process poultry, but there are actually many ways, and you can customize your methods to suit your needs.

Here are a few things to think about when considering the method that you choose:

- Do you want to save the giblets?
- Do you want to package your birds as whole chickens or pieces?
- The processing method should always be done in a way that prevents contamination with feces or undigested food from the crop. This is why we fast our chickens for at least 24 hours before processing.

If you plan on saving the giblets, ensure you have an extra container to place them in while processing. You should also have a waste container for the organs, such as the intestines. For the purpose of this book, we'll be discussing how to process birds into whole frozen chickens step by step.

Step 1

Once you've made sure that the bird is rinsed and clean, you can start by removing the head. Using a sharp knife, start cutting right under the beak and cut through to remove the head. You can place the head in your waste container.

Step 2

Take the foot of the chicken in one hand and bend it at the knuckle. Make an incision in the little valley between the two joints and remove the foot. Do this with the other foot as well.

Step 3

On top of the tail of the chicken, you'll see a little bump. This is called the oil gland. Chickens use their beaks to spread oil from the oil gland along their feathers, making it water resistant. This oil gland should be removed, as it can taint the meat if it comes in contact with it. To remove the oil gland, place your knife well behind the bump, cut downwards, and then toward the end of the tail, *scooping* the oil gland out.

Step 4

Placing the chicken on its back on a surface, pinch a piece of skin between your fingers just above the breast at the beginning of the neck. Lift the skin and make a small cut in the skin only. Use your fingers to pull open the skin toward the neck until the esophagus and windpipe are visible. The esophagus should be empty, so you can use your hand to pull it out from the opening that you've made. Place it in the waste container.

Step 5

The next part involves gutting the chicken. Keeping the chicken on its back, position it so that the legs are pointing toward you. Between the bottom of the breast and the vent, you will notice loose skin. You want to pinch that skin between your fingers and pull it upwards. This will put a bit of strain on the skin, making it easier to cut.

Being careful not to cut any intestines, make a cut in the skin large enough for two of your fingers to fit through. Place one finger under the bottom of the breast inside the hole and the other finger toward the vent. Pull open the skin carefully, making the hole large enough to pull out the organs with your hands without puncturing them.

Step 6

Reach into the opening with your hand and gently start breaking the connective tissue that holds the organs in place inside the carcass. Feel around the sides and sever them with your fingers, once again being very careful not to rupture anything. Start pulling out the organs as you sever the connective tissue.

The lungs will most likely stay behind after you've removed the other organs. You can reach in and pull them out, too. There is a small greenish organ near the chicken's liver. It is the gallbladder filled with bile, so make sure not to puncture it. If you accidentally puncture it, the bile will make the meat bitter. To avoid this, rinse it off immediately. Using your fingers, you can gently sever whatever giblets you want to keep and throw the rest in the waste container.

Step 7

You'll notice that the only part still attached to the chicken is the intestine that leads to the vent. You don't want to cut this open, so you will have to be careful. Make two cuts, one on each side of the vent. Use your knife to cut under the intestine, as to cut out the intestine completely.

Step 8

All you have left to do is to thoroughly rinse and clean the bird. You can do this using a hose and rinsing out the inside of the carcass until the water runs clean. Ensure that you clean the outside thoroughly as well.

You can now place your chicken in an ice bath. It's important to leave the chicken in the ice bath for enough time to allow it to cool down properly. Three to four hours should do the trick, but you can also leave them overnight if you have enough space.

Step 9

After your chickens have been chilled thoroughly, you can package them in your desired packaging. If you're using shrink bags, you can use your scalding pot or turkey fryer and fill it with water.

There will usually be an indication on the packaging of the shrink bags that you choose of how warm the water should be, but a good rule of thumb is to heat it to around 180°F. Place the chicken inside the bag and dip it into the warm water. The bag will shrink around the chicken, and you should always try to push out as much air as possible in order to preserve the meat for longer.

Remember to keep the dipping time as short as possible to not heat the chicken up again, but make sure the shrinking process has finished before removing it. Place a zip tie securely around the top of the bag, and cut off the excess plastic. It's a good idea to use freezer-safe labels and markers to write any relevant information, such as slaughter date and weight, on the bag. Once you've finished with this step, your chickens are ready to go into the freezer!

DELICIOUS CHICKEN RECIPES FOR YOUR HARVEST

As someone who has always been intimidated by cooking chicken, I had to go and find some recipes that didn't scare me as much and learn many lessons in the process. Cooking your own home-grown chicken meat is one of the most satisfactory experiences you can get on the homestead. Your own chicken meat will taste immeasurably better than supermarket meat, and that's a guarantee.

Whole Roasted Chicken

This recipe is a simple few-ingredient recipe that can really impress. Sometimes, less is more, and it's exactly that with this recipe. You can pair this chicken up with some rice and veggies cooked in your preferred way or anything that you like serving with chicken. You don't have to use the seasoning that I'm recommending, and you can get creative with yours. You can add any seasoning that you like with chicken, and your chicken will still turn out great.

Prep time: 5 minutes.

Cook time: 1 hour and 30 minutes.

Ingredients: Salt, pepper, paprika, 1 tsp minced garlic, 1 whole chicken weighing around 5 lbs with the legs trussed, dried oregano, and olive oil—enough to coat the entire chicken.

Directions:

1. Preheat your oven to 425°F.
2. Pat your chicken dry with some kitchen paper to ensure no moisture is left on the chicken.
3. Rub the oil onto the chicken, making sure that you coat it thoroughly.
4. Season the chicken with the garlic, paprika, salt, pepper, and oregano. You can use an amount that suits your taste for each of these.
5. Place the chicken inside an oven tray and into the oven.
6. You can check on the chicken every 3o minutes, and around the 70-minute mark, you can place a thermometer into the middle of the thigh to see if it is the right temperature. It should be around 165°F. The total cooking time will depend on the size of your chicken. If the chicken is smaller, it will cook faster, meaning that you can check a few minutes earlier. Larger chickens will take longer to cook.
7. Remove the chicken from the oven and let it cool down for 10 minutes before cutting. Serve and enjoy!

Chicken Supreme

If you enjoy saucy, creamy chicken dishes, this one's for you. I love this dish because you can pair it up with so many things. You can impress friends and family with this dish and show them how tasty organic chicken can be. You can add more bacon and garlic if you like.

Prep time: 5 minutes.

Cook time: 40 minutes.

Ingredients: 2 chicken breasts with skin, 50 g bacon strips, 50 ml white wine, 1 tbsp butter, ½ tbsp Dijon mustard, 150 ml heavy cream or double cream, 1 tsp crushed garlic, 1 tsp plain flour, 1 tsp olive oil, 1 onion or scallion sliced, salt and pepper to taste, and herbs for seasoning.

Directions:

1. Caramelize the onion or scallop in a frying pan with the butter and oil. This will take around 10 minutes. Add salt to taste and the garlic. Fry the bacon with the onions until cooked. Once everything is done, place it into a separate dish.
2. Season your chicken with salt and pepper and herbs of your choice. Fry it in the same pan over medium heat for

about 8 minutes on the skin side and 5 minutes on the other side. The skin should be crisp and brown. Think chicken breasts may take a bit longer on each side to cook through.

3. Once your chicken is cooked, you can reheat the bacon and onion with the chicken in the pan. Add the flour and stir thoroughly for a few minutes. Thereafter, you can add the white wine. Seethe or simmer for 5 minutes.

4. Lower the heat of the stove and add the cream and Dijon mustard. Ensure that the skin side is facing up, and leave it on the stove for 5 minutes. Take a bite and enjoy!

Tasty Drumsticks

There is nothing tastier than a well-cooked drumstick. You can pair these drumsticks with some healthy home-grown stir-fried vegetables, cooked vegetables, or pretty much anything else that you enjoy from your garden. Feel free to modify the seasoning for this recipe to taste.

Prep time: 5 minutes.

Cook time: 45 minutes.

Ingredients: 1 tbsp olive oil, salt and pepper to taste, 1 tbsp butter, 1 tsp garlic powder, 1 tsp dried basil, ½ tsp paprika, and 2 lbs of drumsticks.

Directions:

1. Preheat your oven to 425°F.
2. Coat the drumsticks thoroughly with olive oil and add seasoning. You can toss the drumsticks to ensure they are properly coated with all the seasoning.
3. Place your seasoned drumsticks in a non-stick baking tray or line a baking tray with foil, and place in the oven.
4. When 20 minutes have passed, turn all the drumsticks.
5. Bake for another 20–25 minutes, and remove from the oven.
6. Place the drumsticks in a bowl and coat with melted butter.
7. You can optionally add some more seasoning and coat again with butter. Sever immediately.

PRESERVATION METHODS FOR CHICKEN MEAT

Most farmers choose to preserve their chicken meat by freezing, which is also the method that I prefer. However, this leaves us to rely on our freezers, and power outages or any other issues with electricity leave us at risk of losing all of our produce. This is why it's always a good thing to have a few backup methods of preservation. Before trying to preserve any chicken meat, remove the skin and any fat. Fat doesn't keep well and may become bitter and cause your meat to spoil faster.

Chicken meat should be canned using a pressure canner. However, it's highly important that you use proper canning techniques and recipes. Without them, you are at risk of contracting *botulism*, "a bacterial-induced condition caused by toxins."

These toxins are produced by the bacteria *clostridium botulinum* and are deadly to humans. You should never take chances with canned chicken, and if you've never canned anything before, consider trying with something easier such as fruits or vegetables.

Canning chicken meat will allow you to stock up the pantry with food and be prepared for any situation. You will also be able to save some space in the freezer with this method. You can use canned chicken in a few recipes, and contrary to what most may believe, it is actually quite tasty and very tender.

Chicken meat can be placed in the can, cooked or partially cooked. This is referred to as hot packed or raw packed. You can leave the bones in, but I've found it easier to use boneless chicken meat. You can add some seasoning to your chicken before canning, which will make the final product a bit tastier.

Another preservation method that you might consider is drying. This can be done using a food dehydrator. Chicken meat should be cooked thoroughly before dehydrating, as this will prevent harmful bacteria from surviving. You can use canned chicken or pressure cook your chicken. This will ensure that the meat is not too tough when dried.

Before placing the chicken in the dehydrator, ensure that you remove all of the excess moisture by pressing down on it with a paper towel on a flat service. The chicken will take about 8 hours to dehydrate and should be done at 145°F (Mallory, n.d.).

Once again, ensure you remove all the skin and fat to make your chicken last longer. Overall, thorough research is impeccable when trying other preservation methods than freezing. The USDA website will be able to give you a lot of helpful information that you can use to successfully store your produce.

CHAPTER 4
INTEGRATING CHICKENS INTO YOUR LIFESTYLE AND COMMUNITY

The only ethical decision is to take responsibility for our own existence and that of our children. –Bill Mollison

Chickens can do so much more for you than provide you with meat and eggs. There are so many ways to incorporate them into your daily life and truly make use of all of the benefits they can provide you with. Throughout this chapter, we'll explore how feathery friends can benefit us in everyday life and how to use them to our advantage.

THE HOMESTEAD ECOSYSTEM: CHICKENS AND BEYOND

The ultimate goal is to become more self-reliant and live a sustainable life. Nature has so much to offer, and ensuring that we're treating it with respect will yield so much more in the long run. Farming doesn't only have to benefit you and your family. Contrary to popular belief, it can benefit the environment around you as well, and in doing so, it can increase your yields in more than one area of your homestead.

The purpose of a homestead is to help its owner live a more sustainable lifestyle and to become less dependent on other establishments for daily needs, such as food. This can include growing your own vegetables, raising your own animals, and producing your own resources such as electricity.

A homestead is a perfect example of why balance is so important. Many backyard chicken farmers have limited space in which they can produce their own resources. This means that they have to take advantage of everything that nature can offer them in a small space. If there is no balance in a homestead, you can easily exhaust your resources.

Permaculture is "a concept that explains how we can mimic the natural movement and actions in an ecosystem to help it thrive while keeping it healthy and producing a high yield." Nature works exactly as it was designed to, and if we can mimic nature, we're ensuring that everything serves its true purpose. This will automatically help keep things in balance. The idea is to work with nature instead of against it.

PERMACULTURE PRINCIPLES APPLIED TO BACKYARD CHICKEN RAISING

Permaculture can be applied to almost any operation that you can think of, and backyard chicken farming is no different! By applying permaculture principles to your farming operation, you can effectively reduce your labor and improve your yield at the same time. The 12 principles of permaculture were created by Bill Morrison and David Holmgren and have since been studied by many others (Manner, 2020).

E. Waddington lists the following 12 principles of permaculture (Waddington, 2019):

1. Observe and interact.

2. Catch and store energy.
3. Obtain a yield.
4. Apply self-regulation and feedback.
5. Use and value renewables.
6. Produce no waste.
7. Design from patterns to details.
8. Integrate, don't segregate.
9. Use small, slow solutions.
10. Use and value diversity.
11. Use edges and value the marginal.
12. Creatively use and respond to change.

Observe and Interact

The first principle is probably the most important of all. This part usually happens before we have even started with our project and continues to apply throughout everything.

Observation is a powerful tool if you know how to use it. Observe what nature does, and try mimicking it and working with it. For instance, observe where the sun falls in the space that you want to use. If you want to ensure that the coop will get some additional warmth, use this observation to build a coop that will take advantage of the sunshine.

You can also save yourself some trouble and observe things such as weather patterns and adjust your coop design and farming practices in a way that will accommodate these patterns.

The first principle is not only applied to the space that you use but also to the people around you. We can learn a lot from observation. You can pick up many skills by observing the practices that other backyard chicken farmers implement on their property.

Observing things like local predators will also give you an idea of what type of coop and protection you will need for your animals. Permaculture principles are so amazing because we implement so many of them on a daily basis without even knowing it. If we can implement it intentionally, we can do so much more and get so much more from our projects.

Catch and Store Energy

By using every little bit of energy that nature has to offer, we save ourselves the trouble of having to create new sources of energy later. Using the same example as above, you can catch and store energy in your coop by designing it in a way that will ensure extra heating from the sun.

Preservation is a great part of this principle. For instance, it takes a lot of energy from your animals to produce eggs and meat, and if it goes to waste, so does that energy. The moment we start preserving our produce, we're also preserving energy.

You can catch and store solar energy by making use of solar lights or any other solar electricity system. You will need to make an initial investment to get the system into place, but once you have it, the possibilities of catching and storing energy are endless. Collecting rainwater is also a great form of catching and storing energy.

Obtain a Yield

Obtaining a yield from your backyard chickens can mean so much more than eggs and meat. This principle teaches us that we shouldn't invest in empty work. Once you see that the yield you're getting isn't enough, you should go back and reevaluate your entire system and use the other principles in permaculture to see how you can improve it to a point where the yield is worth it.

Your yield can also be emotional. To me, backyard chicken farming relieves stress and gives me happiness. I see this as an emotional yield that I'm reaping from my chickens. Another yield you should consider is the skills you develop from backyard chicken farming.

Apply Self-Regulation and Feedback

Being honest with yourself is vitally important to the success of your project. It may sound simple, but in reality, we all live in denial sometimes. This principle involves admitting when you've made mistakes and correcting them in the future.

When something goes wrong, it can be easy to blame everything and anyone else. Sometimes, our own actions can cause big problems, and if we're not honest with ourselves about them, we can easily make the same mistake in the future.

We should constantly be evaluating ourselves and our actions in everything we do. It's okay to make mistakes because we learn from them, but the problem comes in when we shift the blame instead of learning. Mistakes are naturally eliminated in nature. Evolution is a great example of this, and *survival of the fittest* is the main idea. We should, like nature, self-regulate when something doesn't work and adjust to the environment.

Use and Value Renewables

Instead of using resources that are easily depleted, like fossil fuels, permaculture steers us into a more sustainable approach to farming. Going green is the ultimate answer to self-reliability, and if you take good care of your environment, your environment will take good care of you.

Plants you can grow in your own garden can replace depletable feed sources. Plants such as sunflowers, clover, and buckwheat can replace the need to buy them in the store. Remember to keep the nutritional needs of your chickens in mind when doing so.

Produce No Waste

Permaculture is all about ensuring that you get the most out of everything, even the waste. Chicken manure is a fantastic fertilizer and can be composted with old bedding to add to your garden. Chicken manure is rich in many nutrients and minerals that your plants need to thrive in any case.

In Chapter 2, we learned that chickens, especially hens that produce eggs, need calcium in order to produce good-quality eggs. You can reduce the waste that you produce by crushing eggshells very finely and adding them to the chicken feed. Crushed eggshells can also be added to the garden to provide your plants with some essential minerals.

When it comes to this principle, you can get very creative. The smallest change, such as throwing the old water—that you're about to replace in the water bowls of your animals—into the garden, makes a difference.

Design From Patterns to Details

This permaculture principle deals with everyday patterns that take place in our environment and behavior. When designing your coop and working space, keep simplicity in mind.

Once again, this is a great example of where the first principle comes in handy. By observing your daily behavior, you can determine the best way to organize things around your coop for your own convenience. For instance, ensure that the water source that you need for your chickens is close to the coop and easily accessible.

These small design elements make a massive difference in the amount of labor you need to complete your daily tasks. This ties back in with the second principle of catching and storing energy. Your labor takes valuable energy every day, and conserving as much energy as possible with simple tasks will allow you to do much more with your time.

If you have a garden, you can observe the patterns of the insect life and other creatures that roam the environment and implement those observations into your project. If you see that certain pests are plaguing a part of your garden, you can use your chickens for natural pest control and design your routine with them according to that. An example of this may be letting your chickens *graze* daily in a certain part of the garden where there is a pest problem.

Integrate, Don't Segregate

This principle is all about working with all of the elements that have an impact on the project rather than against them. A great example of this will be staying up to date with health problems in the flocks near yours and working with other chicken farmers in the area to protect the health of your animals. Sharing valuable skills and information with other farmers will also benefit the entire local poultry system and help you improve your knowledge and skills.

As mentioned in the previous principle, chickens can be used for pest control. Chemical pesticides are bad for the environment and can cause harm to the animals and even beneficial insects in the garden. Working with nature will entail using natural pest control, like your chickens, instead of poisoning everything in your little ecosystem with chemicals. Companion planting with pest-repellant plants is also a great option.

Keep in mind that chickens do have a taste for a few of your yummy vegetables, so you will need to protect some of them with netting or anything else that will prevent your chickens from chowing down on them. While your chickens are helping you get rid of some pests, they will also fertilize the soil with their manure.

Use Small, Slow Solutions

When jumping right into a project without careful consideration and thought, you run the risk of wasting a lot of resources. We all love starting new hobbies, but not all of us love carrying through with them.

It's completely human to start something exciting and new, just to feel overwhelmed in the middle of it, and consider quitting entirely. To prevent this, it's better to start out small with your project and learn valuable lessons along the way than to invest massively into something and end up wasting the resources if you don't follow through.

Chicken farming is intimidating, especially if you don't have a lot of experience. Consider starting out with a few grown hens to get the feel of it before throwing your all into it.

A problem that often arises with modern farming is the desire to find an immediate solution to every problem. Natural solutions take time to work, but chemicals and other artificial solutions give us a *quick fix*, often at the expense of our health or the health of our flock. To make chickens grow faster, antibiotics are sometimes given to them instead of nutritious, high-quality feed. Antibiotics may make the animals produce faster, but they're very unhealthy for the animals and us.

The quick fix might seem exciting and easy, but, in reality, it takes away a lot more than it gives. When applying this principle to your project, just remember that longer-lasting solutions, more often than not, take longer to achieve.

•   •   •

Use and Value Diversity

As the saying goes, *don't place all your eggs in one basket*. There are many ways in which this permaculture principle can be implemented into your chicken farming project and your life in general. This principle serves to show us how important diversity is on the homestead.

Nature is full of diversity, and your homestead should be no different. Even when starting out small, try to make use of diversity as much as possible. You can try planting some vegetables while raising your chickens, even if that wasn't your original plan.

In farming, diversifying the different streams of income is a great idea, as your farm will still be able to move forward even if one of the operations fails. In terms of a backyard chicken operation, you can apply this principle by diversifying your solutions to certain problems. Let's call it the ultimate *plan B, C,* or even *D!* This may include having different options for processing your chicken, or even diversifying their food sources.

Ensuring that you have different options in terms of where you can get equipment that you need or medicine for your animals is another way of valuing diversity. Consider buying chicks at different times instead of all at once. If you're raising your chickens for meat, this will help you achieve a continuous harvest. You can also diversify your breeds and the ages of your layers.

Use Edges and Value the Marginal

In nature, we often see that edges between two ecological habitats show outstanding growth and production. This is referred to as the *edge effect*. Where the ecological habitats merge, the benefits of both of the habitats are present in one area.

When designing the layout of your project, you can take advantage of this concept by making use of edges. I plant insect-attracting plants at the edges of my chicken run, which provides my chickens with a few extra treats and foraging opportunities.

Creatively Use and Respond to Change

Change isn't always a bad thing, and can sometimes give you a few extra opportunities regarding your backyard chicken farming project. Change pushes us to become more adaptable and resilient. In today's life, we can't afford to stay the same. As our world is constantly changing, we should strive to be flexible enough to be able to keep up.

The trick is to observe the change in time and respond accordingly. When things are out of the norm, such as the climate or our production, we should be ready to face them. If you notice a change in production, you can go back over your principles and start working on changes that will bring your production back to where it needs to be.

Chicken farming strategies have changed so much over the years and will forever keep changing. We change how we do things as we learn, which is an amazing trait that humans have picked up from nature and others around us. This helps us grow when we need to, learn when we need to, and even make mistakes when we need to. In all of this, we should always strive to be better than yesterday and learn a little bit more from others around us.

HOW TO USE CHICKEN WASTE FOR COMPOSTING AND GARDENING

Chicken manure creates some of the best compost on the market, in my opinion. You'll find that most of the essential nutrients and minerals that plants need to thrive are present in chicken manure. Why buy compost when you can make your own with any waste from your chickens? You can save money and reduce your waste at the same time by using manure and bedding to create nutrient-rich compost for your garden.

Not only is this type of fertilizer great for your plants, but it's also so much better for the environment than artificial fertilizer. If applied correctly, you can expect a good yield and an improved soil biome, which will, in turn, further improve your production and yield in the garden.

You can use any waste produced by your chickens in your home-made compost. This includes bedding material, food scraps, egg shells, and even some feathers lying around! As chicken manure contains high amounts of nitrogen, it should be composted prop-erly before applying it directly to your garden, or it may cause your plants to become *burnt*. Chickens that forage between plants don't usually produce enough manure in one spot to cause this problem.

There are a few ways in which you can create compost with chicken manure, of which the most popular is using a compost bin or box. These can be found at most gardening outlets or on Amazon. You can also create your own by recycling an old plastic trash can or anything similar which has a lid.

Furthermore, you can create a compost pile, but be mindful of the smells that it may cause. Your neighbors might not enjoy the smell of composting chicken manure. In general, any composting project should be done far away enough from your home and those of your neighbors to not cause unpleasant smells in your living spaces.

When creating your own compost, you should know the difference between *brown* and *green* waste. *Brown waste* refers to "more woody materials and plants that have died some time ago, usually not containing a lot of moisture." *Green waste* refers to "things like green plants and other fresher compostables."

In general, brown waste consists of things that have a dry consis-tency and are more woody. In general, brown waste consists of things that have a dry consistency and are more woody. Chicken manure falls under green waste, while old bedding materials fall under brown waste.

The optimal ratio is usually between three and four parts brown waste to every one part of green waste (Van der Linden, 2022). You can add the waste to your compost bin or a compost pile. Ensure that your compost is always moist but never wet and soggy. Within a couple of days, your compost will produce heat in the center.

A compost pile should be created in layers. The first layer will be brown waste. Wet the first layer and place a layer of green waste. Thereafter, you can add another layer of brown waste. Adding some soil to your compost pile is also beneficial. You can repeat the process until you've added all of your waste.

You can mix and turn your compost at most once a day or at least every two days while keeping it moist. The heat produced will help destroy any unwanted bacteria or weed seeds. Your compost should be ready within about three weeks from the first day (Harvill, 2023).

CHICKENS AND COMMUNITY: SHARING YOUR JOURNEY

The community plays a crucial role in backyard chicken farming and chicken farming in general. Chicken farming can be daunting for beginners, which is why sharing knowledge is so important. One of the main goals should include helping others in your community to also become more self-reliant and self-sustainable.

A community that depends less on large commercial farms is a stronger community overall. By sharing knowledge and experiences with your local neighbors, you're building a more resilient community. If you're farming to sustain your family, you can help others do the same by encouraging them to do the same.

This is a great way to keep wealth local and stop helping large commercial farms make more money. If you're raising chickens to sell their produce, you can play a key role in the local economy.

With all the benefits that raising backyard chickens holds, not sharing these ideas and practices with your neighbors will be such a shame. The chicken farming communities in most areas are usually quite tight-knit, as farmers discuss how they can improve biosecurity and the overall health of their flocks with one another.

Even if you only have a few chickens or a small project, the health of all of the flocks in your area should be a concern for you. There is a possibility that your flock might be compromised if the health of flocks near you is compromised. This makes it even more vital to stay up to date with everything going on in your local community.

Because other flocks near you have an influence on your flock's well-being, ensuring that you share all valuable lessons and skills that you pick up with your community is vitally important. A community that sticks together thrives together.

Many of the lessons that I have learned throughout the years came from local homesteaders that have become close friends of mine. It is always possible to learn something from others, and knowledge is priceless, which is why no one can take it from you.

IDEAS FOR ENGAGING NEIGHBORS, CREATING A CHICKEN-RAISING COMMUNITY

Maintaining good relationships with your local community, even non-farmers, is paramount when it comes to the success of your project. We should always be considerate of others, especially our neighbors. The goal is to engage others, even if they're not farmers themselves, and to educate them on our practices. This will make them a lot more understanding and can make the future of our project a lot more comfortable.

As we've discussed, there are many different regulations in different neighborhoods, areas, zones, states, and countries on backyard chicken farming. You can petition to turn laws to your advantage by having a good relationship with your neighbors, and you may be able to make them a little more lenient where you need it. Neighbors who understand your operation and feel like they are a part of it are much more likely to vouch for you and speak in your favor.

Apart from engaging non-farmers in the community, focus should also be placed on engaging experts in the field, as well as beginners. A great way to do this is by joining or forming social media platforms where information can be shared about your journey, and you can learn a lot from others as well.

Most areas will have existing platforms for such groups, so make sure you ask around locally to find out where you can join them. Sharing success stories and your personal journey can encourage others to also start their own projects and encourage other farmers to continue with theirs.

Joining social media pages and groups is probably the easiest way to engage with others in the community, and you'll also be able to find information on seminars, workshops, and community events. I always say that there is no such thing as too much information, so joining as many of these as you possibly can will benefit you greatly. Moreover, you can encourage others to do the same and build a stronger, more knowledgeable community in the process.

Once you're comfortable with your project, you can consider hosting a gathering for the community to come and learn about your project. Joining and hosting mentorship programs will also do a great deal for you and the community. Learn about local festivals and fairs and how you can participate to spread awareness and education about backyard chicken farming.

Sharing your bounty is a fantastic way to make people aware of the wonders of chicken farming. Whether your goal is to produce for yourself and your family or to generate a profit, there will always be an opportunity to gift neighbors with some of your produce.

Overall, being part of a community in this industry can really make a massive difference in the outcome of your project. Chickens can become loud and produce some odors, which may be something that concerns your neighbors. By ensuring that you treat your neighbors with respect and do everything you can to cause as little inconvenience to them as possible, you can maintain a healthy relationship with them.

CHAPTER 5
THE FUTURE OF BACKYARD CHICKEN RAISING

To me, there's nothing more special than providing food for other families, and that's what we do out here. –Wanda Patsche

Adaptability is more important than ever in the day and age that we live in, and all change doesn't have to be bad. Technology is forever changing and improving, and there are so many ways in which we can incorporate it into our backyard chicken farming projects. Some believe that traditional chicken raising is the best method, and I tend to agree to a certain extent.

Having said that, I also believe you should take advantage of technology if it can help you make production more efficient and effective without sacrificing good ethics. Even if you decide that you don't want to use certain technologies in your project, it's always good to know about them anyway.

RAISING CHICKENS IN THE DIGITAL AGE

Back in the day, the good old notebook and pen was a chicken farmer's best friend. Keeping track of important information can help you better determine how your project is going and whether you're on the right track or not. Noticing a reduction in production is significantly harder if you don't have records of it, to begin with.

Record-keeping is essential, no matter how you do it. The first principle of permaculture involves thorough observation, and record-keeping can help you master this skill. Here are some of the things that you may want to take note of:

- the date that chickens were bought
- where chickens were bought
- all expenses and income
- growth rate and weights
- egg production
- average egg size and weight
- daily temperatures and overall climate
- feed given
- any illness or disease
- treatments given
- mortalities
- vaccinations
- water intake
- cleaning schedules
- losses due to incidents with predators

If you're like me and you enjoy taking thorough notes of everything, this won't be a problem for you. However, it may be challenging for someone who isn't as keen on doing the administrative part of chicken farming.

Luckily, there is an easier solution. These days, you can get applications on your phone or computer that can help you easily track all or most of these things. Some applications are very sophisticated and will allow you to track mountains of information in one place. Other applications will give you the basics, and for some farmers, that's all they need.

A big concern to many flock owners when it comes to digital tracking of the flock is losing all of their data. Let's be honest, technology isn't perfect, and there is always a risk. However, most applications and programs now connect to an online cloud, which means that even if your device is damaged, you will still be able to access your information through another device.

Before placing all of your trust in an application or program, ensure that you make backups of all of your information regularly. You can also double-check whether your data is being automatically backed up to a cloud or not.

One such application is called *Flockstar*. This application can help you track egg production, note each chicken and all of its information, including photos, track expenses, and more. Other honorable mentions include *Poultry Master* and *My Poultry Farm*.

There is such a variety of applications and programs that you can use that it might seem a bit overwhelming to choose one. Keep your goals in mind, and determine which information you need to track to reach them. This will give you a better idea of which application will suit your needs.

On the other hand, some poultry farmers prefer buying fertilized eggs and incubating them themselves. While this is a great way to do things, buying an incubator can be quite costly. However, if you want to incubate many eggs and buying an incubator is an investment worth making for your project, there are many options to choose from. There is also the option of creating your own incubator or buying one second-hand.

You will find very sophisticated and automated incubators on the market, which will make the entire incubation process much easier for you. Eggs need to be turned a few times a day while in the incubator, and the temperature and humidity should be constant.

Automatic incubators take care of the turning for you and also keep the temperature and humidity at the optimal level. You're guaranteed a better hatching rate, and your labor is significantly reduced.

The advancements in technology in the chicken farming industry are insane, and there are a lot of high-tech systems being used all over the world. Some of them include behavior monitoring sensors, highly sophisticated automatic feeders and drinkers, as well as automated lighting systems. In spite of the fact that these seem very fun and interesting, it may be a bit overkill to use them in the backyard flock.

ONLINE RESOURCES AND COMMUNITIES FOR CHICKEN RAISERS

You will find chicken farming online communities on almost any social media platform that you can think of. Blogs are also a great resource for you in your journey, as backyard chicken farming bloggers share their personal experiences and advice.

Joining groups on messaging services and platforms like *Facebook* can really make a difference. You can ask for advice and have your questions answered freely on most social media platforms, and it's also a great way to stay up to date with all of the new technology and equipment going around in the chicken farming community.

You will also be able to share your personal experiences, which may encourage others online to follow in your footsteps. Personal experiences are extremely valuable and carry so much weight in this community. As always, there is a lot to learn from others.

Here are some blogs and websites that I would highly recommend to any chicken farmer:

- *The Chicken Chick*, otherwise known as Kathy Shea Mormino, is an avid backyard chicken farmer who shares all of her experiences and lessons on her blog. I personally enjoy reading her content, as it's very informative yet personal. I would say that she is one of the people that has inspired me to do a lot more with my project.

- "The Spruce" is just a fantastic website overall, which is run and edited by experts in their respective fields. This website will provide you with countless information on chicken farming, gardening, and even everyday household tips. I've been following this website for a while, and I've not been disappointed for one second.
- "Community Chickens" is a fantastic resource, as the information on this website is provided by a few different people with experience in chicken farming from all over the United States. You will find so much helpful information here, and the website is very easy to navigate.
- "The Prairie Homestead" is a blog run by Jill Winger, and it is more than just informative. She goes through many topics that every homesteader will appreciate. I would say that this is a great information source if you're looking to go into homesteading.
- "Our Inspired Roots" is also another great homesteading blog, which I would recommend. You'll find some more resources on books and other helpful topics on this blog.
- "Raising Happy Chickens" is a very comprehensive website that includes all kinds of helpful information for chicken farming, and the website itself is very well organized, making it easy to navigate.

These days, we don't have to rely solely on reading for our information. Sometimes, we need to see something done before we have the confidence to attempt it ourselves. This is where YouTube comes in. There is no shortage of helpful videos pertaining to backyard chicken farming and homesteading, and you'll learn mountains of information when doing the right search.

Here are a few channels that I would recommend watching:

- "Next Level Homestead" is a relatively new YouTube channel which started out in 2021. On this channel, you'll find a lot of information on backyard chicken farming, homesteading, gardening, and so much more. This channel is highly personable, and I could watch these videos all day!
- If you're looking for some wholesome, informative, and helpful videos on homesteading and farming in general, "Stoney Ridge Farmer" is a YouTube channel that will suit those needs. They focus on regenerative and sustainable farming, which is a great way to do things. You won't regret subscribing to this channel.
- While homesteading is becoming more and more popular, not everyone has a lot of space to spare. "Epic Homesteading" is a YouTube channel that's all about urban homesteading, and I would highly recommend subscribing. I've been following this channel for a few years, and I've learned so much in the process. If you want to know how to get your sustainable homestead going in an urban environment, including your backyard chicken project, this channel is the one for you.
- "Acres of Adventure" is a homesteading YouTube channel that covers a wide variety of topics, including raising chickens. This is a great channel for beginners to watch.

With so many online resources for chicken farming and homesteading, we should always be careful to only follow advice from bloggers and YouTubers if we can validate their credibility. You don't want to put all of your hard work and your entire project at risk by following uncredible advice and false information.

RESILIENCE AND INDEPENDENCE IN AN UNCERTAIN WORLD

THE ROLE OF CHICKEN RAISING IN ENHANCING PERSONAL AND COMMUNITY RESILIENCE

Raising chickens is more than just a hobby. Even though it's very rewarding in many ways and can be done for fun, it has the potential to change entire communities. We all know the feeling of being dependent on someone. Whether it's a parent or a partner, at some stage in your life, you were dependent on someone for something.

Once you're dependent on someone else for something, it can feel like you've lost control of the situation. You have to constantly look into the eyes of someone else to meet your needs. If something goes wrong with your supply, you have no backup plan. You're left at the mercy of the producers.

Not only can you be dependent on someone else for essential daily needs such as food, but you can also become emotionally dependent on them. Your livelihood is not in your own hands. Not knowing whether your needs will be met is something that you'll have to think about constantly. Once again, the power is in the hands of the producers.

This is what it can be like to be dependent on large-scale commercial farms for your daily essentials. You're forced to pay their asking price, no matter how ludicrous it can be, because you have no other choice.

By raising your own chickens, you're taking your livelihood back into your own hands. You're building a personal resilience that can't be broken down by rises in prices or limited stock. When things get ugly in the poultry industry, you'll still have everything you need in that regard.

Instead of placing your hope and trust in large-scale farms that don't really care about your individual situation, take things into your own hands and ensure that you can meet your own needs. Place your trust in your community, people who know you personally and actually care whether you have what you need or not.

Communities have so much power that they don't know about. If only everyone could understand what whole communities are capable of, we would see a massive change in how things are done.

LOOKING FORWARD: THE FUTURE OF URBAN HOMESTEADING AND POULTRY FARMING

I honestly believe that homesteading and backyard chicken farming are the future. When we look at how many people are starving all around the world due to the price of food and just the lack thereof overall, we can see exactly what kind of dire situation we're in.

We always say, "It won't happen to me." We live our comfortable lives, giving away wealth to large-scale commercial farms while we don't even notice what's going on around us. You may not know this, but people often don't know it when they're struggling. People close to you might be a victim of the rising prices in the food industry, and you won't even know it.

We're heading toward an uncertain place in the future where we can either accept all of the chaos happening around us or make our own plans. More and more people are realizing how horrific the food industry is becoming and turning toward homesteading.

By producing your own food, you're keeping the wealth in your community instead of throwing it into the pockets of already billionaires. I believe homesteading will become somewhat of a norm, where we will turn back to the skills that we once left behind and look toward a healthier, more sustainable future.

Imagine a community of people who believe that they should put their own first and live a healthier and more connected lifestyle. Imagine the connections and relationships that can be made throughout the community by sharing this invaluable information. I believe strongly that more people should be encouraged to take on this lifestyle and that it could turn an uncertain future into a beautiful, healthy one.

There will be many more advancements in techniques and technology in the coming years, and I find it very exciting. If we look at how things have changed in the past few years, it's almost unimaginable to think about what the next chapter holds for chicken farmers. Let's work on our combined resilience. As Henry Ford once said, "If everyone is moving forward together, then success takes care of itself."

CONCLUSION

EMBRACING INDEPENDENCE: THE PATRIOT'S JOURNEY

When all is said and done, progress is what matters in all areas of life. Whether we do it fast or slowly, whether it's easy or hard, we should always focus on progress. Backyard chicken farming enables us to progress in the right direction when it comes to self-sustainability and -improvement. When we move in this direction, we're setting ourselves up for current and future success. We take back the power into our own hands and become an active part of a better world and community.

We should be ready for massive changes in the future because they *are* coming. There is no way to know how they will affect our lives and resources, and all we can do is prepare ourselves. It's clear to see that things simply can't stay the same when looking at the changes we've had only in the past 5–10 years.

Food is becoming more dangerous, chemical-ridden, and expensive by the day. We simply can't sit by and watch how large corporations are poisoning us and our loved ones. There has never been a time when it has been as important as now to learn new skills and become less reliant on other sources.

Even the environmental impact of large commercial chicken farms would have been enough to convince me, but the economic and personal benefits of backyard chicken farming just add more fuel to the flame. Backyard chicken farming remains a symbol of resilience and independence, and I would encourage anyone seeking these things to start out with chickens.

Choosing the right breed for your homestead is so important. If you choose the wrong breed and it does not live up to your goals, you might see it as a failure, whereas in reality, a more careful consideration of which breed you want to keep would have given you much better results.

Before choosing a breed for your homestead, remember to consider the following things:

- What are your production goals?
- Is the breed suited to your climate and environment?
- Do you have the means necessary to give the breed everything it needs to thrive?
- Have you done enough research on the challenges that you may face when it comes to a specific breed?
- Will its temperament suit your situation?

Once you've chosen a breed, you can start looking at housing options. You'll find a very helpful list of resources as to where you can find a few different options for your homestead in the

"Resources for Chicken Raising Supplies" section at the end of the book.

Whatever option you choose for housing, it should always be able to keep your chickens safe, warm, and comfortable. Housing can be one of the most expensive initial investments, depending on if you buy or build your own coop.

The next thing you'll have to consider is nutrition for your flock. Your chickens have some basic needs that will have to be met, regardless of what brand of feed you choose to feed them. The following nutrients are important to keep in mind:

- protein
- carbohydrates
- vitamins and minerals
- fats
- dietary fiber

Your chickens will have different needs for each of these categories depending on their age, breed, production stage, and individual bodies. I recommend using trustworthy organic feed and supplementing whatever they might need additionally. On top of their nutritional needs, your chickens will always need access to clean, fresh water. Without water, nothing can survive. Water is truly the essence of life itself.

Chickens left to forage and graze will need grit to aid their digestion. Grit is used to help mince up feed into smaller parts inside the crop, which allows the food to move to the stomach and be further digested. There are two types of grit: insoluble and soluble. Soluble grit is made from sea shells and can be used as an additional calcium source, whereas insoluble grit is made from granite or flint and is merely passed through the digestive system.

You will have to choose between medicated and unmedicated feed. Medicated feed can have an influence on vaccines that you may have given your chickens, so it's always important to double-check whether it's safe. I prefer unmedicated feed that will allow your chickens to become stronger and more resilient on their own.

In any operation that involves raising animals, you will most definitely come across health problems at one stage or another. There are ways to be prepared, but unfortunately, there is no way to eliminate them completely. Knowing what you can expect can make your journey a lot easier.

Chickens can face some of the following health problems:

- parasites
- wounds
- bacterial infections
- viruses

Having a good cleaning system in place can help you reduce these problems. You should ensure that your chickens always have clean feeders and drinkers and that their coop is sanitary and clean. Change bedding regularly and ensure that you check their manure often, as many health issues can be spotted early when looking at the manure.

Biosecurity is crucial when it comes to keeping the flock healthy. Try to reduce contact with wild birds and animals to a minimum, as they can carry diseases that may affect your flock. When you've visited places that have a lot of wild birds, don't come into contact with your flock until you've taken a good shower and changed your clothes.

Be careful to use equipment from other poultry farms, as it may also be a source of contamination for your flock. Keep your own equipment clean at all times, and don't invite other poultry farmers to your project without caution. Always stay up to date with the neighboring chicken farmers about health conditions on their farms, and try to learn from them as much as you can.

Vets play a significant role in the health of chicken flocks. As many health conditions can affect chickens, which are contagious to other flocks as well, you should never take chances. Respiratory issues, as well as sudden unexplained deaths, should be reported to your local vet or authorities immediately.

Vets are generally eager to help when it comes to getting some advice on the health of your flock, and if you're ever unsure about something, don't hesitate to give them a call. It's always better to learn from an expert than to play the guessing game.

Chickens are small and vulnerable animals, which makes them an easy target for predators. Predators are a big problem in the industry and can cause many losses if not managed properly. Your coop should be built in a way that will reduce the risk of predators entering.

Ensure that you stay on top of the maintenance of your coop, as any rotten planks or other parts that are run down can be an access point for predators. I like placing fine chicken wire over my ventilation areas to ensure that nothing unwanted can use it as a gateway to my flock.

Some predators are known to dig under chicken runs, so I would recommend burying your fencing at least a foot deep into the ground. If there is a problem with aerial predators in your area, consider covering the top of your chicken run with chicken wire or fine netting. Chicken wire generally isn't strong enough to keep larger predators out, so use some squared galvanized wiring instead. Moreover, keeping the area around the coop clean is impeccable. Any debris will attract predators and give them a spot to hide.

Chickens have a very sophisticated hierarchy, which is called the pecking order. This involves the stronger, larger, and more aggressive birds to be at the top and the weaker or older birds at the bottom. The birds at the top of the pecking order will take on the role of protectors but will also have access to all of the best resources. Chickens will consider their human as part of the pecking order, and some roosters may challenge you for the top spot.

Chickens are very intelligent animals and will watch your behavior as closely as you watch theirs. When a rooster challenges you for the top spot, you shouldn't back down. Be gentle but firm. Something like a broom or a bucket can help you look more intimidating. If a rooster sees that he can dominate you, you'll have a problem on your hands.

Interacting with your chickens on a regular basis is a great way to earn their trust. If you've raised them since chicks, they will be more likely to be comfortable around you. I find that speaking with my chickens and making them used to my voice and movements tend to make them more comfortable as well.

You can teach your chickens to come when called by speaking to them as you interact with them. Don't make any fast or intimidating movements, and always be gentle when handling them. Some breeds love being handled while others aren't quite as fond of it. However, you can earn their trust by giving them snacks and making an effort to spend a lot of time with them.

One of the best parts of chicken farming is collecting your produce. Nothing beats a fresh, organically farmed, healthy chicken egg in the morning! Your brooding boxes should be lined with soft bedding to prevent cracks and breakages in eggs. You can use an egg collector specifically designed for the job to collect your eggs or any container lined with something soft to protect the eggs.

I would recommend storing your fresh eggs in the fridge, as this will make them stay fresh longer. Egg cartons work best, but you can store them in anything that will keep them from rolling around and getting damaged.

Be sure to change bedding in brooding boxes regularly to prevent eggs from becoming dirty with manure. Eggs that are completely covered in manure should be discarded, as they might be contaminated with bacteria. However, if there are a few dirty spots, you can wipe the eggs down gently with a cloth and some water or remove the markings with fine sandpaper.

Meat production is a little bit more tricky, and there are a few things that you should keep in mind when deciding to take that route. Make sure that you know the laws pertaining to the slaughter of your chickens in your area, and check with authorities before you do so.

The age and weight of slaughter will depend on the breed that you choose, as we've discussed in Chapter 3. Here are the main things that you should have in place before processing day:

- adequate storage space in a freezer
- all of the equipment needed
- packaging and labels
- a well-sanitized working area
- fasting your chickens for 24 hours

The first thing that will happen on processing day is dispatching your chickens. This is done by placing the chicken in the restrictive cone and cutting the jugular vein. There will be a reflex action where the nerve endings of the chicken are triggered, but this is completely normal.

After dispatching, the chickens are left in the cone to bleed out and then taken to the processing area. The next step is defeathering, which is done by placing the chicken in a stock pot or turkey fryer with heated water for a while until the feathers are easy to pluck out. Thereafter, the feathers are removed by hand or using an electric plucker.

Once the feathers have been plucked, the chicken can be processed. We've discussed nine steps to do so, but you don't have to do it exactly the same way. There are many ways to do the processing, and there is no one specific way to do it. You can customize your processing method to your specific needs.

After processing, the chickens are placed in an ice bath to cool down and prevent them from thawing in your freezer for a few hours. Once cooled down, they're ready for packaging and freezing.

Chicken meat can be preserved by freezing, canning, or drying. When canning or drying your chicken meat, ensure you use USDA-approved methods and do a lot of research beforehand, as doing it incorrectly can be deadly to your health.

The benefits of keeping don't have to stop at personal benefits and production. Your chickens can be successfully integrated into your homestead and backyard ecosystem by applying the permaculture principles to your farming style.

The environment has a lot to offer us if we treat it with respect. Permaculture is all about letting nature do the work for you and ensuring that we enrich it instead of destroying it. We observe nature and copy its methods. This is the best way to manage your project, in my opinion, as you'll be able to give back to nature in the process of providing for yourself and your family.

In this setting, chicken waste can be used in your gardening to enrich your soil and increase your production. Chicken manure should be composted before applying it to the garden, as it can burn your plants if applied directly. You can compost their manure, bedding, and feed scraps.

Composting can be done in a compost bin or a compost pile. Always remember to keep your compost as far away as possible from your living spaces and neighbors because there might be some initial unpleasant smells.

The community is a very important part of chicken farming, and engaging others will always be one of the best things you can do for yourself and for its members. Keep in touch with other chicken farmers on social media, attend workshops, and organize community events to engage more people in your project. Building resilience is not only important as an individual but also as a community, and engaging others may encourage them to take steps toward sustainability.

On the other hand, everything is becoming digital these days, and chicken farming is no different. There are countless applications and programs in the market which can help you easily keep track of all of the important information regarding your flock. We've looked at a few of them, but don't be shy to explore more options.

Blogs and chicken farming websites are great online resources that we can use to learn more about the project. I've listed a few of my favorites, but there are so many to choose from when doing a quick online search. Remember to check the credibility of the authors before using their information and advice.

TAKE THE RISK, REAP THE REWARDS

At the end of the day, humans are wired to be afraid of change. Even if some of us don't show it, change is scary. However, at the pace that our world is changing, it's something that we have to accept and learn to not only live with but adapt to. If we stay the same in a changing world, we won't survive.

It will be daunting to take on this challenge, but there is no shortage of information and support for new chicken farmers in all of the communities that we've spoken about in this book. We're called to embrace the American spirit of independence and resilience for the sake of ourselves, our families, and our communities.

So much can be accomplished if you gain the right information and confidence. Get yourself into a good support system, and become a part of the chicken farming community before you get started. The amount of care and love, as well as the learning you will experience, is unparalleled.

Everyone starts somewhere. No one is born an expert in anything, and we have to learn to walk before we can fly. You can accomplish anything that you set your mind to, and all that may be keeping you from accomplishing all of your goals is the fear of failure.

There is no such thing as failure if you have learned something from an experience. The only thing stopping you from living a better, sustainable, and secure lifestyle is you! Go ahead and take that first step to take back your security, hope, and freedom. As *The Lorax* once said, "Unless someone like you cares a whole awful lot, nothing is going to get better. It's not." You have the power to create positive change in your hands, and all you have to do now is use it.

SHARE YOUR INSIGHTS

Thank you for choosing to read my book! I hope you enjoyed the journey through its pages. Your feedback and reviews mean a lot to me, and they help others discover our work. If you have a moment, I would be incredibly grateful if you could leave a review on Amazon. Your honest thoughts can make a significant impact.

To access a selection of my other literary works, scan this QR code.

Thank you once again for your support, and I look forward to hearing your thoughts. Happy reading!

RESOURCES FOR CHICKEN-RAISING SUPPLIES

In this section, I'll be presenting to you a few places where you can get your basic chicken-raising supplies. Keep in mind that the type of supplies you need will depend on your unique situation, as we've discussed throughout the book.

- If you want to buy a coop, you can decide whether you want to buy a secondhand coop, a ready-built coop, or a coop kit. You can also use recycled materials to build your coop, but ensure that it's properly cleaned and not hazardous to your animals before you use it.
- "The Shed Yard" is a website that specializes in selling ready-made coops and other farm structures. It has a variety of options, and it also has payment plans such as rent-to-own possibilities if you don't want to pay the balance in full upfront. This option is quite pricey, but it's up to you.
- Good old Walmart has a wide selection of chicken coop options, which are quite affordable. You can find almost any backyard chicken farming equipment there, and I personally buy a lot of mines there.

- Amazon has countless equipment options, especially for galvanized chicken runs and small coops. You'll find feeders, drinkers, feed, and all other kinds of equipment needed.
- *Horizon Structures* has many chicken coop models to choose from and can also do a custom build for you.
- *Chicken Coop HQ* is a company that sells chicken coop kits that are relatively easy to put together.
- *Ace Hardware* sells a wide variety of tools for building and even things like galvanized chicken wire that can help you with your project.
- "eBay" is a great resource for all kinds of chicken supplies.
- "Facebook Marketplace" is one of my favorite places to check for secondhand coops and other building materials that might be needed in building a coop. You can even find other secondhand equipment by doing a quick search.
- "Premier1Supplies" will most certainly have almost anything you need regarding your poultry project. From fencing to incubators, even down to slaughtering knives and equipment, they've got you covered. Their supplies are all organized neatly under four tables, namely incubation, brooding, rearing, eggs, and processing. This makes it very easy to find what you're looking for.
- "My Pet Chicken" has a wide variety of equipment that you will need, especially some specialized chicken-coop cleaning supplies.
- "Stromberg's Chickens" is a website where you'll be able to find some general medicines, vaccinations, and other supplies for your flock.

There are countless resources for chicken farmers out there, and once again, by forming a part of a community, you can also get some resources from other chicken farmers. Before using any resource, ensure it is credible and trustworthy, especially when buying your chicks or fertilized eggs.

RECOMMENDED READINGS FOR FURTHER EXPLORATION

- *Hatching & Brooding Your Own Chicks: Chickens, Turkeys, Ducks, Geese, Guinea Fowl*—Gail Damerow
- *Storey's Illustrated Guide to Poultry Breeds: Chickens, Ducks, Geese, Turkeys, Emus, Guinea Fowl, Ostriches, Partridges, Peafowl, Pheasants, Quails, Swans*—Carol Ekarius
- *DIY Chicken Coops: The Complete Guide To Building Your Own Chicken Coop*—John White
- *DIY Chicken Coops: 12 Chicken Coop Plans That Will Teach You How To Build a Dream Chicken Coop*—Adrienne Witherrell
- *Nutrition and Feeding of Organic Poultry*—Robert Blair
- *The Farm That Feeds Us: A Year in the Life of an Organic Farm*—Nancy F. Castaldo
- *Homemade Chicken Feed: A Complete Guide and Recipe Book for Your Flock*—Allen Priest
- *The Chicken Health Handbook, 2nd Edition: A Complete Guide to Maximizing Flock Health and Dealing with Disease*—Gail Damerow
- *Chicken Health For Dummies*—Julie Gauthier and Robert T. Ludlow

- *What's Killing My Chickens?: The Poultry Predator Detective Manual*—Gail Damerow
- *How to Protect Chickens from Predators: The Complete Guide to keep your Chickens Safe from Coyotes, Raccoons, Foxes, Dogs, Hawks and More*—David Josephson
- *The Behavioural Biology of Chickens*—Christina J. Nicol
- *Poultry Products Processing: An Industry Guide*—Shai Barbut
- *Butchering Chickens: A Guide to Humane, Small-Scale Processing*—Adam Danforth
- *The Homesteading Handbook: A Back to Basics Guide to Growing Your Own Food, Canning, Keeping Chickens, Generating Your Own Energy, Crafting, Herbal Medicine, and More (Handbook Series)*—Abigail Gehring
- *Introduction to Permaculture Design: Transform Your Backyard into an Edible Food Forest Oasis*—Aster W. Green

GLOSSARY

Biosecurity: Measures taken to control the spread of transmissible diseases in the flock (Mandal, n.d.).

Broiler: A chicken raised specifically for meat production.

Broiler house: A structure that is normally heated and created to house chickens that are raised for meat production.

Carbon footprint: The emission of carbon dioxide gas by an individual. *Carbon dioxide* is "a greenhouse gas that contributes to global warming."

Cockerel: A young rooster.

Commercial chicken farming: Large-scale chicken farms owned by corporate enterprises. These farms often use antibiotics, growth hormones, and artificial substances in the poultry farming business.

Crop: An enlarged area of the esophagus used to store food for a period of time before moving to the stomach.

Culling: Selecting specific chickens to remove from the flock.

Dispatch: To humanely kill or put down a chicken that is to be processed.

Docile temperament: A generally calm and non-aggressive temperament.

Eco-friendly: Not harmful to the environment in its production phase or as a finished product. Methods of doing things can also be referred to as eco-friendly if they don't harm the environment.

Embryo: An early-stage developing chicken inside the egg. The embryo will develop into a fetus as time progresses and they grow.

Fast: To take away your chicken's food for a certain amount of time.

Flock: A group of chickens.

Giblets: Edible organs in the chicken, such as the heart, liver, neck, gizzards, and kidneys.

Gizzard: The strong muscle of the stomach in the chicken, which is also considered edible.

Greenhouse gasses: Gasses that contribute to the greenhouse effect and global warming.

Hatchery: A business that specializes in the hatching of chicks.

Chicken insecticides: Chemicals that remove ectoparasites from chickens.

Molting: The act of shedding old feathers and growing new, healthy feathers. This will normally happen once a year.

Non-broodiness: A chicken is referred to as non-broody when they don't have the urge to lay on their eggs for long periods of time.

Organically farmed chickens: Chickens that are farmed in the most natural way possible. Chickens are only fed organic feed, which is fresh and healthy, and they have access to a lot of space to move around in.

Prepper: Derived from the term *doomsday prepper*, the word refers to individuals who stockpile food and other essential supplies in preparation for a future disastrous or cataclysmic event.

Pullet: A young hen, usually between 16 and 52 weeks old (Lesley, 2022a).

Respiratory issues: Problems that chickens may encounter with their lungs or breathing.

Scuffles: Chickens fighting for a higher spot in the pecking order.

Self-sustainability: The ability to provide your own essential needs and sustain yourself with things such as food and water.

Self-reliance: The confidence to rely on yourself for a service or product rather than someone else.

Topical substance: A substance such as an ointment or antibiotic, which is applied directly to an area of the chicken's body.

Truss: Tying the legs of a processed whole chicken together with kitchen twine.

Vent: The anus of the chicken, which serves as an outlet for urine and feces, as well as eggs.

BIBLIOGRAPHY

About chickens. (n.d.). Compassion in World Farming. https://www.ci-wf.org.uk/farm-animals/chickens/

About chickens farmed for meat. (n.d.). Compassion in World Farming. https://www.-ciwf.org.uk/farm-animals/chickens/meat-chickens/

Acres Of Adventure Homestead. (n.d.). Acres Of Adventure [Video]. YouTube. https://www.youtube.com/@AcresOfAdventure/videos

Alexander, G. (2020, July 7). *Chickenomics: The Economics of Backyard Chickens.* Earth-911. https://earth911.com/home-garden/chickenomics-the-economics-of-back-yard-chickens/

All Chicken Coop Kits (Sales Event). (n.d.). Chicken Coop HQ. https://chicken-coophq.com/collections/chicken-coops

American Chemical Society. (2007, April 10). *Arsenic In Chicken Feed May Pose Health Risks To Humans.* Science Daily. https://www.sciencedaily.com/releas-es/2007/04/070409115746.htm

Arcuri, L. (2023, March 9). *All About the Rhode Island Red Chicken Breed* (A. R. Newton, Ed.). The Spruce. https://www.thespruce.com/chicken-breeds-rhode-island-red-3016554

Arsenic. (2018, February 15). World Health Organization. https://www.who.int/news-room/fact-sheets/detail/ar-senic#:~:text=Long%2Dterm%20exposure%20to%20arsenic

Ask UNH Extension. (2019, February 26). *What are the best ways to protect my chickens from predators?* University of New Hampshire. https://extension.unh.e-du/blog/2019/02/what-are-best-ways-protect-my-chickens-preda-tors#:~:text=Burying%20mesh%20at%20least%20one

Australorp Chickens: Everything You Need To Know. (2021, March 10). The Happy Chicken Coop. https://www.thehappychickencoop.com/australorp-chickens-a-comprehensive-care-guide/

Avian influenza (bird flu) fact sheet. (n.d.). KZN Health. http://www.kznhealth.gov-.za/cdc/avianfs.htm

Backyard chicken coop products for sale. (n.d.). eBay. https://www.ebay.com/b/back-yard-chicken-coop/bn_7024861906

Backyard Chickens Part 1: Preparing To Buy Healthy Birds. (2023, March 2). VMBS News. https://vetmed.tamu.edu/news/pet-talk/backyard-chickens-part-1/

Barth, B. (2016, March 16). *The Secrets of Chicken Flocks' Pecking Order.* Modern Farmer. https://modernfarmer.com/2016/03/pecking-order/#:~:text=One%20last%20thing%3A%20Humans%20are

Benton, T. (2023, January 20). *So How Much Space Does a Chicken Really Need?*

Somerzby.   https://www.somerzby.com.au/blog/how-much-space-does-a-chicken-need/#:~:text=If%20your%20chickens%20are%20in

Berry, J. G., & Lester, C. (n.d.). *Home Processing of Poultry.* Pine Valley Central School.   https://www.pval.org/cms/lib/NY19000481/Centricity/Domain/200/Home_Processing_of_Poultry.pdf

Beth. (2023, June 10). *Ranch Chicken Drumsticks.* Budget Bytes. https://www.budgetbytes.com/ranch-chicken-drumsticks/

Biggs, P. (n.d.-a). *Chick Starter Feed: What to Feed Baby Chicks.* Purina Mills. https://www.purinamills.com/chicken-feed/education/detail/chick-starter-feed-what-to-feed-baby-chicks-for-a-healthy-life

Biggs, P. (n.d.-b). *How Long Do Eggs Last and Fresh Egg Facts.* Purina Mills. https://www.purinamills.com/chicken-feed/education/detail/how-long-do-eggs-last-facts-about-farm-fresh-eggs#:~:text=A%20general%20rule%2C%20unwashed%20eggs

Biggs, P. (n.d.-c). *What Can Chickens Eat Chicken Treats to Feed and Avoid.* Purina Animal Nutrition. https://www.purinamills.com/chicken-feed/education/detail/what-to-feed-chickens-chicken-treats-to-feed-and-avoid

Bird flu: what is it and how can you protect your chickens? (n.d.). Raising Happy Chickens.   https://www.raising-happy-chickens.com/bird-flu.html#:~:text=So%20any%20form%20of%20avian

Boggs, N. (2014, October). *American Pastured Poultry Producers Association - Comprehensive Guide to Feeding Grit to Pasture-Raised Chickens, Turkeys, and Poultry.* APPPA. https://apppa.org/feeding-grit#:~:text=Poultry%20will%20only%20eat%20as

Bradford, A. (2016, March 9). *How to turn your oven into a dehydrator.* CNET. https://www.cnet.com/home/kitchen-and-household/dont-have-a-dehydrator-use-your-oven/

Broiler breeder farm. (n.d.). Let's Talk Chicken. https://letstalkchicken.ca/farm-to-table/breeder-farm/#:~:text=They%20will%20lay%20between%20145

Bryan, L. (2023, March 18). *Super Easy Roast Chicken.* Downshiftology. https://downshiftology.com/recipes/easy-roast-chicken/

Butchering Chickens: A Guide to Humane, Small-Scale Processing. (n.d.-a). Amazon. https://www.amazon.com/Butchering-Chickens-Humane-Small-Scale-Processing/dp/1635861659

Butchering Chickens: A Guide to Humane, Small-Scale Processing. (n.d.-b). Amazon. https://www.amazon.com/Butchering-Chickens-Humane-Small-Scale-Processing/dp/1635861659

Caroline's Homestead. (2021). Leghorn Chickens: Everything You Need to Know About the Breed! [Video]. YouTube. https://www.youtube.com/watch?v=t6a_xUCfKq0

Caughey, M. (n.d.-a). *Cold-Weather Chickens for Chilly Climates.* HGTV. https://www.hgtv.com/outdoors/gardens/animals-and-wildlife/cold-weather-chickens-for-chilly-climates#:~:text=Three%20docile%2C%20cold%20hardy%20breeds

Caughey, M. (n.d.-b). *How to Keep Your Chickens Safe.* HGTV. https://www.hgtv.com/outdoors/gardens/animals-and-wildlife/how-to-keep-your-chickens-safe

Home Canning and Botulism. (2023, June 5). CDC. https://www.cdc.gov/foodsafety/communication/home-canning-and-botulism.html

Cherian, G. (2015). Nutrition and metabolism in poultry: role of lipids in early diet. *Journal of Animal Science and Biotechnology, 6*(1). https://doi.org/10.1186/s40104-015-0029-9

Chicken and Poultry Supplies. (n.d.). Premier 1 Supplies. https://www.premier1supplies.com/c/poultry-supplies/

Chicken coops. (n.d.). Amazon. https://www.amazon.com/s?k=chicken+coops&crid=11JG5SFULLDPT&sprefix=chicken+coops%2Caps%2C401&ref=nb_sb_noss_1

Chicken Coops in Chickens. (n.d.). Walmart. https://www.walmart.com/browse/pets/chicken-coops/5440_7335155_3985092?adid=22222222254456653014&wmlspartner=wmt-labs&wl0=&wl1=g&wl2=c&wl3=642814712286&wl4=dsa-2090118833405&wl5=1028679&wl6=&wl7=2840&wl8=&veh=sem&gclid=Cj0KCQjwz8emBhDrARIsANNJjS7y0yjb7auqE6RqE-9s_00vltydtGxNtLAuDlu3Ow-ENDguU-tmTDvoaAtjjEALw_wcB

Chicken Health For Dummies. (n.d.). Wiley. https://www.wiley.com/en-us/Chicken+Health+For+Dummies-p-9781118460986

Chicken Waterer: Which Type Does Your Flock Need?. (2022, July 25). The Happy Chicken Coop. https://www.thehappychickencoop.com/chicken-waterer/

Clark, E. (n.d.). *Chicken supreme.* BBC Good Food. https://www.bbcgoodfood.com/recipes/chicken-supreme

Cluck cluck girl. (2016, December 9). *The Art Of Socializing Chickens.* BackYard Chickens. https://www.backyardchickens.com/articles/the-art-of-socializing-chickens.72460/

Commercial Poultry Definition. (n.d.). Law Insider. https://www.lawinsider.com/dictionary/commercial-poultry#:~:text=Commercial%20Poultry%20means%20poultry%20wholly

Community Chickens. (n.d.). https://www.communitychickens.com/

Compost Basics Part 2: The Nitty-Gritty. (2018, June 18). Brown's Greens. https://brownsgreens.net/compost-basics-part-2-the-nitty-gritty/#:~:text=%E2%80%9CGreen%E2%80%9D%20materials%20are%20new%2C

Conde, G. (2023, February 10). *Leghorn Chicken Breed: Everything You Need To Know.* Eco Peanut. https://www.ecopeanut.com/leghorn-chicken/

Conley, M. (2018). *45 quotes that celebrate teamwork, hard work, and collaboration.* HubSpot. https://blog.hubspot.com/marketing/teamwork-quotes

Considering Rhode Island Red chickens? The 19 things you must know first. (n.d.). The Featherbrain. Retrieved June 24, 2023, from https://www.thefeatherbrain.com/blog/rhode-island-red-chickens#:~:text=The%20commercial%20strains%20of%20Rhode%20Island%20Red%20are%20much%20smaller

Coop Cleaning. (n.d.). My Pet Chicken. https://www.mypetchicken.com/collections/cleaning

Coops, B. C. (2020, June 26). *First Few Days and Weeks with Baby Chicks*. Backyard Chicken Coops. https://www.backyardchickencoops.com.au/blogs/learning-centre/first-few-days-and-weeks-with-baby-chicks

Countryside Contributor. (2019, December 2). *Blue and Black Australorp Chicken: A Prolific Egg Layer*. Backyard Poultry. https://backyardpoultry.iamcountryside.com/chickens-101/blue-and-black-australorp-chicken-a-prolific-egg-layer/

Crank, R. (2022, August 17). *3 of The Best Dual-Purpose Chicken Breeds*. Backyard Poultry. https://backyardpoultry.iamcountryside.com/chickens-101/3-of-the-best-dual-purpose-chicken-breeds/#:~:text=Best%20Dual%2DPurpose%20Chicken%20Breeds%3A%20The%20Speckled%20Sussex&text=The%20Speckled%20Sussex%20chicken%20is

Crude Fat in Layer Nutrition. (2017, August). Lohmann Breeders. https://lohmann-breeders.com/crude-fat-in-layer-nutrition/#:~:text=Fat%20must%20be%20present%20in

Cruz-Rincon, S. (2021). *Common Bacterial Diseases in Backyard Chickens*. Veterinary Partner. https://veterinarypartner.vin.com/default.aspx?pid=19239&catId=102911&id=10048768

Damerow, G. (2015, December 29). *The Chicken Health Handbook, 2nd Edition: A Complete Guide to Maximizing Flock Health and Dealing with Disease*. Storey Publishing LLC.

Daniels, T. (2009, August 21). *Temperament of Different Chicken Breeds*. Poultry Keeper. https://poultrykeeper.com/keeping-chickens/temperament-of-different-chicken-breeds/

Davis, T. (2022, October 27). *Best Meat Chickens for Homesteading*. The Imperfectly Happy Home. https://www.imperfectlyhappy.com/best-meat-chickens-for-homesteading/

Department of Health - RHP&R - Health Protection - Food Safety and Regulation. (2020, June 22). Better Health Channel. https://www.betterhealth.vic.gov.au/health/healthyliving/keeping-backyard-chickens

Developer, F. (n.d.). *About Flockstar*. Flockstar App. https://www.flockstarapp.com/

Dibble, L. (n.d.). *13 Best Homesteading Bloggers of 2022*. Hillsborough Homesteading. https://hillsborough-homesteading.com/top-homesteading-blogs-of-2019/

DIY Chicken Coops: 12 Chicken Coop Plans That Will Teach You How To Build a Dream Chicken Coop: (Keeping Chickens, Raising Chickens For Dummies, ... Guide to Raising Backyard Chickens) - Witherell, Adrienne: 9781519429131 (n.d.). Abe Books. https://www.abebooks.com/9781519429131/DIY-Chicken-Coops-Coop-Plans-1519429134/plp

Drinkers for hens: which ones to choose. (2022, May 26). River Systems. https://www.riversystems.it/en/which-drinkers-for-hens-to-choose/

Dumas, S. E., Lungu, L., Mulambya, N., Daka, W., McDonald, E., Steubing, E., Lewis, T., Backel, K., Jange, J., Lucio-Martinez, B., Lewis, D., & Travis, A. J.

(2016). Sustainable smallholder poultry interventions to promote food security and social, agricultural, and ecological resilience in the Luangwa Valley, Zambia. *Food Security, 8*(3), 507–520. https://doi.org/10.1007/s12571-016-0579-5

Easy Broccoli-Cheese Eggs in a Mug Recipe. (2019, July 9). . Eat This Not That. https://www.eatthis.com/broccoli-cheese-eggs-mug-recipe/

El-Gazzar, M. (2022, October). *Mycoplasma gallisepticum Infection in Poultry.* Veterinary Manual; MSD Veterinary Manual. https://www.msdvetmanual.com/poultry/mycoplasmosis/mycoplasma-gallisepticum-infection-in-poultry

Embryology of the chicken. (n.d.). Poultry Hub Australia. https://www.poultry-hub.org/anatomy-and-physiology/body-systems/embryology-of-the-chicken

Epic Homesteading. (n.d.). *Home* [YouTube channel]. YouTube. https://www.youtube.com/@epichomesteading/featured

Espinosa, R. A. (2019, August). *Cystic Right Oviduct in Poultry.* MSD Veterinary Manual. https://www.msdvetmanual.com/poultry/disorders-of-the-reproductive-system/cystic-right-oviduct-in-poultry

Ezenwankwo, S. (2023, April). *Healthy and Ethical: Organic Chicken Benefits.* Poultry Farm Guide. https://www.poultryfarmguide.com/blog/why-choose-organic-chicken/

Factors affecting nutrient requirements. (n.d.). Kansas State University. https://www.asi.k-state.edu/extension/swine/swinenutritionguide/general_nutrition_principles/factorsaffectingnutrientrequirements.html

Facts about avian influenza in humans. (2023, February 8). European Centre for Disease Prevention and Control. https://www.ecdc.europa.eu/en/avian-influenza-humans/facts#:~:text=It%20remains%20poorly%20adapted%20to

Facts about fat. (2022, February 23). NHS. https://www.nhs.uk/live-well/eat-well/food-types/different-fats-nutrition/#:~:text=Eating%20too%20much%20saturated%20fats

Fairchild, B. D. (2005, August 8). *Basic Introduction to Broiler Housing Environmental Control.* The Poultry Site. https://www.thepoultrysite.com/articles/basic-introduction-to-broiler-housing-environmental-control

Fanatico, A. (2003, January 10). *Feeding Chickens for best health and performance.* The Poultry Site. https://www.thepoultrysite.com/articles/feeding-chickens-for-best-health-and-performance

Farm Life. (2021, October 31). *150 Best Quotes About Agriculture and Farming.* AgFuse - Agricultural Social Network. https://agfuse.com/article/150-best-quotes-about-agriculture-and-farming

Fewell, A. K. (2021, July 17). *Broiler Chicken Breeds: 16 of the Best Meat Chickens.* The Fewell Homestead. https://thefewellhomestead.com/broiler-chicken-breeds-16-of-the-best-meat-chickens/

Fincher, M. (2022, April 3). *What Are Chicken Gizzards and How Do You Cook Them?* Allrecipes. https://www.allrecipes.com/article/what-are-chicken-gizzards/

Fisher, S. (2023, June 27). *15 DIY Compost Bin Plans* (A. R. Newton, Ed.). The Spruce. https://www.thespruce.com/compost-bin-plans-4769337

Ford, C. (2022, July 20). *Herbs and Spices That Go With Chicken*. Amli Residential. https://www.amli.com/blog/herbs-and-spices-that-go-with-chicken

Garden Craft 24 in. H X 25 ft. L Galvanized Steel Poultry Netting 1 in. (n.d.). Ace Hardware. https://www.acehardware.com/departments/building-supplies/gates-and-fences/chicken-wire/70791?gclid=Cj0KCQjwz8emBhDrARIsANNJj-S49QREgUHPApz2bb78_QbbmCkae-2HEXPuyOyZpUizMVGtWCzQh2p0aAp-GpEALw_wcB

Garman, A. J. (2021, August 24). *How to Compost Chicken Manure*. Backyard Poultry. https://backyardpoultry.iamcountryside.com/feed-health/how-to-compost-chicken-manure/

Garman, J. (n.d.). *Chicken Disease and Illness in Your Flock*. Timber Creek Farm. https://www.timbercreekfarmer.com/chicken-disease-illness-flock/

Gautam, P. (n.d.). *Fat metabolism: can improve poultry performance*. Engormix. https://en.engormix.com/poultry-industry/articles/fat-metabolism-can-improve-t43116.htm

Gehring, A. (n.d.). *The Homesteading Handbook: A Back to Basics Guide to Growing Your Own Food, Canning, Keeping Chickens, Generating Your Own Energy, Crafting, Herbal Medicine, and More (Handbook Series)*. Skyhorse.

Gennetta, N. (2021, February 20). *The Black Australorp: Australia's World Record Egg Layer*. Heritage Acres Market LLC. https://www.heritageacresmarket.com/black-australorp/#:~:text=As%20they%20originated%20in%20Australia

George. (2012, April 11). *Patriotic Duty To Raise Chickens!* Independence Homestead. https://independencehomestead.com/2012/04/10/patriotic-duty-to-raise-chickens/

Glenn. (n.d.). *Dehydrating Chicken*. Backpacking Chef. https://www.backpackingchef.com/dehydrating-chicken.html

Good Food Team. (n.d.). *Healthy egg & chips*. BBC Good Food. https://www.bbcgoodfood.com/recipes/healthy-egg-chips

Guide to giblets. (2021, December 1). Farmison & Co. https://www.farmison.com/community/blog/what-are-giblets

Hale Family Homestead. (2020). How To Butcher Chicken...From Start To Finish! [Video]. YouTube. https://www.youtube.com/watch?v=S8N0R73vLgw

HappyChicken. (2022, February 8). *Poultry Processing Equipment (Everything You Need to Butcher Chickens)*. The Happy Chicken Coop. https://www.thehappychickencoop.com/poultry-processing-equipment-everything-you-need-to-butcher-chickens/

Harvill, J. (2023, July 18). *Chicken Manure: Turning Waste Into Quality Fertilizer*. Epic Gardening. https://www.epicgardening.com/chicken-manure/#:~:text=A%20popular%20%E2%80%9Cquick%2Dheat%E2%80%9D

Hendley, A. J. (n.d.). *Drying Foods*. New Mexico State University. https://pubs.nmsu.edu/_e/E322/

Herrity, J. (2023, February 4). *52 Thought-Provoking Quotes on Managing Change Effectively*. Indeed. https://www.indeed.com/career-advice/career-development/quotes-on-managing-change

Hess, T., & Griffer, M. (2018, February 28). *Daily Diet, Treats and Supplements for Chickens*. The Open Sanctuary Project. https://opensanctuary.org/chicken-diet-and-supplements/

Hojnacki, J. (2012). *The Lowdown on Layers: Top 5 Laying Chicken Breeds and 12 Tips*. Manna Pro. https://www.mannapro.com/homestead/bid/124918/The-Lowdown-on-Layers-Top-5-Laying-Chicken-Breeds-and-12-Tips

Holzer, D. (2023, June 29). *What Does Eco-Friendly Mean?* Weekand. https://www.weekand.com/home-garden/article/ecofriendly-mean-18033627.php

Homemade Chicken Feed: A Complete Guide and Recipe Book for Your Flock. (n.d.). Amazon. https://www.amazon.com/Homemade-Chicken-Feed-Complete-Recipe-ebook/dp/B0BT78D5TK

Hoole, J. (2018, September 25). *Curious Kids: how can chickens run around after their heads have been chopped off?* The Conversation. https://theconversation.com/curious-kids-how-can-chickens-run-around-after-their-heads-have-been-chopped-off-103701#:~:text=This%20is%20called%20a%20%E2%80%9Creflex

Hotaling, A. (2020, September 30). *Lighting Helps Chickens Produce Eggs In Winter*. Hobby Farms. https://www.hobbyfarms.com/lighting-chickens-coop-winter-egg-production/

Hotaling, A. (2023, June 21). *These Apps Can Help You Manage Backyard Chickens*. Hobby Farms. https://www.hobbyfarms.com/these-apps-can-help-you-manage-backyard-chickens/

How Long Does Shrinkbagged Poultry Stay Fresh in The Freezer. (2018, March 28). Poultry Shrink Bags. https://www.poultryshrinkbags.com/single-post/2018/03/28/how-long-does-frozen-poultry-stay-fresh-in-poultry-shrink-bags

How to Build a Compost Pile: Complete Guide with 9 Methods. (n.d.). Planet Natural. https://www.planetnatural.com/composting-101/making/compost-pile/#:~:text=Put%20down%20a%20thin%20layer

How to Can: A Beginner's Guide to Canning Food. (n.d.). Ball. https://www.ballmasonjars.com/canning-and-preserving-101.html

How to Deal With a Violent Chicken or Rooster. (2022, August 9). Nature's Best Organic Feeds. https://organicfeeds.com/how-to-deal-with-a-violent-chicken-or-rooster/#:~:text=You%20should%20attempt%20to%20stand

How To Dehydrate Chicken. (n.d.). Your Adventure Coach. https://youradventure-coach.com/how-to-dehydrate-chicken/

How to Process Chickens At Home. (n.d.). *Chicken Whisperer*. https://chickenwhisperermagazine.com/health-and-wellness/how-to-process-chickens-at-home

Howell, M. (2020, February 3). *The Chicken Whisperer: how to start composting chicken manure*. The Poultry Site. https://www.thepoultrysite.com/articles/how-to-start-composting-chicken-manure#:~:text=To%20start%2C%20collect%20the%20manure,%C2%B0F)%20as%20they%20decompose.

Hudson, J. (2023, April 26). *Red Ranger Chicken: Eggs, Height, Size and Raising Tips*. Chicken Scratch. https://cs-tf.com/red-ranger-chicken/

Jacob, J. (n.d.-a). *EXTERNAL PARASITES OF POULTRY – Small and backyard poultry.* Poultry Extension. https://poultry.extension.org/articles/poultry-health/external-parasites-of-poultry/

Jacob, J. (n.d.-b). *FEEDING CHICKENS FOR EGG PRODUCTION IN SMALL AND BACKYARD FLOCKS – Small and backyard poultry.* Poultry Extension; University of Kentucky. https://poultry.extension.org/articles/feeds-and-feeding-of-poultry/feeding-chickens-for-egg-production/#:~:text=Laying%20hens%20require%20large%20amounts

Jacob, J. (2018, May 15). *Nutrient Requirements of Organic Poultry.* EOrganic. https://eorganic.org/node/7888#:~:text=The%20level%20of%20egg%20production

Jamie. (n.d.). *Homesteading Books: Your Guide to 30 of the Absolute Best.* Why Farm It. https://whyfarmit.com/homesteading-books/

Jennifer. (2019, June 7). *How much protein do Chickens need?* Dine a Chook. https://www.dineachook.com.au/blog/how-much-protein-do-chickens-need/

Jess. (2023, February 17). *Organic Eggs vs Regular Eggs – what's the difference?* Honestly Kitchen. https://honestlykitchen.ie/2023/02/17/organic-eggs/#:~:text=Studies%20have%20suggested%20that%20while

Josephson, A. (2023, March 20). *The Economics of Raising Chickens.* SmartAsset. https://smartasset.com/personal-finance/the-economics-of-raising-chickens#:~:text=Another%20advantage%20to%20raising%20chickens

Josephson, D. (2017, December 26). *How to Protect Chickens from Predators: The Complete Guide to keep your Chickens Safe from Coyotes, Raccoons, Foxes, Dogs, Hawks and More | Paperback.* CreateSpace Publishing.

Justin. (2015, March 25). *Get More Out of Your Chickens (with less work) - Nine Crazy Simple Design Concepts.* Abundant Permaculture. https://abundantpermaculture.com/get-more-from-chickens-less-work/

Kim, J. (2023, June 13). *15 Best Meat Chicken Breeds (With Pictures).* Pet Keen. https://petkeen.com/best-meat-chicken-breeds/

Kirby, S. (2023, August 4). *The Lorax Quotes to Make You Think.* Everyday Power. https://everydaypower.com/the-lorax-quotes/

Kosher King Day Old Meat Chickens. (n.d.). Purely Poultry. https://www.purelypoultry.com/kosher-king-chickens-p-1436.html

Lachlel, M. B. (n.d.). *Tips on Feeding Broilers.* Pets on Mom. https://animals.mom.com/tips-feeding-broilers-4152.html

Lapingcao, C. (2021, July 27). *Chicken Processing 101: When to Slaughter Chickens, Steps & Equipment.* The Happy Chicken Coop. https://www.thehappychickencoop.com/chicken-processing-know-when-to-slaughter-your-chickens/

Large Chicken Coop Models | Prefab Chicken Coop Kits. (n.d.). Horizon Structures. https://www.horizonstructures.com/compare-our-chicken-coop-models?gclid=Cj0KCQjwz8emBhDrARIsANNJjS42CcsKtqRb7Pcb9nMGwfN7m0LcYTUolNaZMIx5JXdkxz1wbKTCHcAaAv7JEALw_wcB

Lee, C. H. (2019, March 5). *How to Turn Our Garden's Bounty Into Community.* Catapult. https://catapult.co/stories/gardening-community-bartering-storytelling-backyard-politics-christine-hyung-oak-lee

Leghorn Chickens. (n.d.). Oklahoma State University. https://breeds.okstate.edu/poultry/chickens/leghorn-chickens.html#:~:text=Characteristics

Lehr, A. (2022, June 16). *The Difference Between Medicated vs Non-Medicated Chick Feed.* Grubbly Farms. https://grubblyfarms.com/blogs/the-flyer/medicated-vs-non-medicated-chick-feed#:~:text=Cons%20of%20Medicated%20S-tarter%20Chick%20Feed&text=It%20can%20only%20be%20used

Lesley, C. (2020, July 18). *Australorp: Egg Laying, Colors, Characteristics And More...* Chickens & More. https://www.chickensandmore.com/australorp/

Lesley, C. (2021, January 17). *The Complete Guide To Chickens And Water.* Chickens & More. https://www.chickensandmore.com/chickens-and-water/

Lesley, C. (2022a, January 12). *What is a Pullet: What to Know Before Buying One.* Chickens & More. https://www.chickensandmore.com/what-is-a-pullet/#:~:text=A%20pullet%20is%20a%20young

Lesley, C. (2022b, June 13). *Common Chicken Health Problems.* Old Farmer's Almanac. https://www.almanac.com/common-chicken-health-problems

Lesley, C. (2022c, June 25). *What Is Chicken Grit? All You Need To Know.* Chickens & More. https://www.chickensandmore.com/what-is-chicken-grit/

Liu, M., Wang, B., Osborne, C. P., & Jiang, G. (2013). Chicken Farming in Grassland Increases Environmental Sustainability and Economic Efficiency. *PLoS ONE, 8*(1). https://doi.org/10.1371/journal.pone.0053977

Lobermeier, K. (2022, July). *How to Butcher and Process Chickens.* Under a Tin Roof. https://underatinroof.com/blog/2022/8/22/how-to-butcher-and-process-chickens

Lorenzoni, G. (2020, October 21). *Crop Disorders of Chickens I: Crop Impaction.* PennState Extension. https://extension.psu.edu/crop-disorders-of-chickens-i-crop-impaction#:~:text=The%20crop%20is%20an%20enlarged

Lorenzoni, G. (2023, March 27). *Management of Coccidiosis in Small Flocks.* PennState Extension. https://extension.psu.edu/management-of-coccidiosis-in-small-flocks#:~:text=One%20of%20the%20easiest%20ways

Macklin, K., & Hess, J. (2022, June 12). *Nutrition for Backyard Chicken Flocks.* Alabama Cooperative Extension System. https://www.aces.edu/blog/topics/farming/nutrition-for-backyard-chicken-flocks/#:~:text=During%20phase%201%20(20%20to

Maclean, K. (n.d.). *The Best Way to Properly Store Freshly Laid Eggs.* Pete & Gerry's. https://peteandgerrys.com/blogs/field-notes/backyard-hens-proper-egg-storage#:~:text=How%20to%20store%20fresh%20eggs

Mallory. (n.d.). *How To Dehydrate Chicken.* Your Adventure Coach. https://youradventurecoach.com/how-to-dehydrate-chicken/

Mandal, A. (n.d.). *What is Biosecurity?* (S. Roberston, Ed.). News-Medical.net. https://www.news-medical.net/health/What-is-Biosecurity.aspx

Manner, L. (2020, September 11). *How the 12 Principles of Permaculture can transform your garden (and our world)*. Green Connect Illawarra. https://green-connect.com.au/heres-your-guide-to-the-12-principles-of-permaculture/

Martin, W., Schuft, A., Porter, R., Noll, S., & Cardona, C. (2022). *Avian influenza basics for urban and backyard poultry owners*. University of Minnesota Extension. https://extension.umn.edu/poultry-health/avian-influenza-basics-noncommercial-poultry-flock-owners#prevent-spreading-disease-between-neighbors-825963

McClellan, M. (2019, October 10). *A Beginner's Guide to Canning*. Serious Eats. https://www.seriouseats.com/how-to-can-canning-pickling-preserving-ball-jars-materials-siphoning-recipes

McCrea, B., & Baker, B. (2022, November 2). *Common Backyard Chicken Behaviors*. Alabama Cooperative Extension System. https://www.aces.edu/blog/topics/farming/common-backyard-chicken-behaviors/

Mccune, K. (n.d.). *How To Pluck Chickens Without A Plucker!* Family Farm Livestock. https://familyfarmlivestock.com/how-to-pluck-chickens-without-a-plucker/

McDermott, T., & Titchenell, M. (2018, December 20). *Predators of Poultry*. Ohioline. https://ohioline.osu.edu/factsheet/vme-22#:~:text=Chicken%20flocks%20are%20often%20more

McMahon, M. (2023, June 23). *What is a Hatchery? (with pictures)*. All Things Nature. https://www.allthingsnature.org/what-is-a-hatchery.htm

Mealeatey, M. (2021, January 20). *Why Failing to Prepare Means Preparing to Fail*. Cambodianess. https://cambodianess.com/article/why-failing-to-prepare-means-preparing-to-fail#:~:text=According%20to%20Benjamin%20Franklin%2C%20%E2%80%9Cby

Merriam-Webster. (n.d.). *Prepper*. Merriam-Webster Dictionary. https://www.merriam-webster.com/dictionary/prepper

Mini Urban Farm. (2022). *How to Butcher a Chicken for Beginners [GRAPHIC]* [Video]. YouTube. https://www.youtube.com/watch?v=hMR5SXKaKsU

Minimum Protein Needs For Chickens. (n.d.). Chicken Heaven on Earth. https://www.chickenheavenonearth.com/minimum-protein-needs-for-chickens.html

Mock, S. (2013, August 21). *Raising Cornish Cross Chickens for Meat*. Purely Poultry Blog. https://www.purelypoultry.com/blog/raising-cornish-cross-chickens-for-meat/#:~:text=The%20Cornish%20Cross%20are%20typically

Monitoring birds as they bleed-out. (n.d.). Humane Slaughter Association. https://www.hsa.org.uk/electrical-waterbath-stunning-of-poultry-bleeding/monitoring-birds-as-they-bleed-out

Morishita, T. Y. (1996). Common Infectious Diseases in Backyard Chickens and Turkeys (from a Private Practice Perspective). *Journal of Avian Medicine and Surgery, 10*(1), 2–11. https://www.jstor.org/stable/30134169

Mormino, K. S. (n.d.-a). *Hatching & Brooding Your Own Chicks by Gail Damerow, Book Review*. The Chicken Chick. https://the-chicken-chick.com/hatching-brooding-your-own-chicks-by/

Mormino, K. S. (n.d.-b). *Backyard Chicken Keeping Information and Advice*. The Chicken Chick. https://the-chicken-chick.com/

Mormino, K. S. (n.d.-c). *Why Water is Critically Important to Chickens*. The Chicken Chick. https://the-chicken-chick.com/why-water-is-critically-important-to/#:~:text=%E2%80%9CWater%20is%20involved%20in%20every

Mormino, K. S. (2014, June 12). *Chicken Anatomy: The Crop, Impacted Crop & Sour Crop*. The Chicken Chick. https://the-chicken-chick.com/chicken-anatomy-crop-impacted-crop-sour/#:~:text=A%20chicken

Moulting in poultry. (2022, November 22). Queensland Government. https://www.business.qld.gov.au/industries/farms-fishing-forestry/agriculture/animal/industries/poultry/health/moult#:~:text=Moulting%20in%20chickens%20and%20other

Murray McMurray Hatchery - Jumbo Cornish X Rock. (n.d.). McMurray Hatchery. https://www.mcmurrayhatchery.com/jumbo_cornish_x_rocks.html

Murray's Big Red Broiler. (n.d.). McMurray Hatchery. https://www.mcmurrayhatchery.com/big_red_broiler.html#:~:text=Murray

Nafea, H. H. (2022, April 11). *Organic chicken and its importance in the nutrition and health of the community*. Agriculture College. https://www.uoanbar.edu.iq/AgricultureCollege/English/News_Details.php?ID=1175#:~:text=Organic%20chicken%20meat%20contains%20more

Nair, D. P. (2022, September 20). *Just Like Puppies and Kittens, Young Chickens Like to Play Too*. Sentient Media. https://sentientmedia.org/young-chickens-play-study/#:~:text=But%20a%20recent%20study%20in

Nettles Cutter, C., & Bucknavage, M. (2023, August 4). *Let's Preserve: Meat and Poultry*. Penn State Extension. https://extension.psu.edu/lets-preserve-meat-and-poultry

News From The Farm. (2021, December 1). Farmison & Co. https://www.farmison.com/community/blog/what-are-giblets#:~:text=The%20giblets%20are%20the%20edible

Newcastle disease - DAFF. (n.d.). Australian Government, Department of Agriculture. https://www.agriculture.gov.au/biosecurity-trade/policy/australia/naqs/naqs-target-lists/newcastle#:~:text=Newcastle%20disease%20only%20affects%20birds

Next Level Homestead. (n.d.). *Home* [YouTube channel]. YouTube. https://www.youtube.com/@NextLevelHomestead/featured

NIFA Staff. (n.d.). *USDA's Complete Guide to Home Canning*. National Institute of Food and Agriculture. https://www.nifa.usda.gov/about-nifa/blogs/usdas-complete-guide-home-canning

Novikova, A. (n.d.). *5 Best Poultry Management Apps for Android & iOS*. Free Apps for Me. https://freeappsforme.com/poultry-management-apps/

9 Big benefits of keeping chickens as pets. (n.d.). Woofpurnay Veterinary Hospital. https://www.woofpurnayvet.com.au/benefits-of-keeping-chickens#:~:text=Keeping%20chickens%20is%20one%20of%20the%20easiest%20ways%20to%20live

Nutrition. (n.d.). Poultry Hub Australia. https://www.poultryhub.org/all-about-poultry/nutrition

Nutrition and Feeding of Organic Poultry 2nd Edition. (n.d.). Amazon. https://www.amazon.com/Nutrition-Feeding-Organic-Poultry-Robert/dp/1786392984

Oliver, J. (n.d.). *Easy cheese omelette recipe.* Jamie Oliver. https://www.jamieoliver.com/recipes/eggs-recipes/simple-cheese-omelette/

Organic Chicken. (n.d.). Plukon Food Group. https://www.plukon.com/farming-concepts/organic-chicken/#:~:text=Organic%20poultry%20meat%20comes%20from

Our Inspired Roots. (n.d.). https://ourinspiredroots.com/

Overview of Greenhouse Gases. (n.d.). United States Environmental Protection Agency. https://www.epa.gov/ghgemissions/overview-greenhouse-gases

Patrick. (2022, May 4). *Chicken Seasoning Blend.* Allrecipes. https://www.allrecipes.com/recipe/174452/chicken-seasoning-blend/

Pendergrass, K. (2018, August 4). *Arsenic in Animal Feed: The Good News and the Bad News.* Paleo Foundation. https://paleofoundation.com/arsenic-in-animal-feed/#:~:text=While%20arsenic%20it

PennDutch. (2019, July 29). *Chicken Coop Buying Guide: What To Know Before Buying.* Penn Dutch Structures. https://www.penndutchstructures.com/blog/chicken-coop-buying-guide/#:~:text=At%20the%20bare%20minimum%2C%20the

Pentagon Pets. (n.d.). *How To Raise And Care For Big Red Broilers Chicken.* Pentagon Pets. https://pentagonpets.com/how-to-raise-and-care-for-big-red-broilers-chicken-2304-xxs/#:~:text=Aggressiveness%20is%20one%20of%20the

Permaculture Design Principle 10: Use and value diversity. (2013, January 8). Permaculture Principles. https://permacultureprinciples.com/permaculture-principles/_10/

Permaculture principles. (n.d.). Brighton Permaculture Trust. https://brightonpermaculture.org.uk/permaculture/permaculture-principles/#:~:text=Permaculture%20was%20originally%20co%2Dcreated

Pieper, A. (n.d.). *The Complete Guide to Sun Drying Fruits and Vegetables.* MorningChores. https://morningchores.com/sun-drying/

Pietsch, M. (2022, June 11). Insoluble fiber - An essential nutrient for poultry. *Feed & Additive Magazine.* https://www.feedandadditive.com/insoluble-fiber-an-essential-nutrient-for-poultry/

Pitesky, M. (n.d.). *6 Most Common Chicken Diseases | Symptoms and Remedies.* Manna-Pro. https://www.mannapro.com/Top-6-Chicken-Diseases

Poultry & Chicken Shrink Bags for Processing Poultry. (n.d.). Flavorseal. https://flavorseal.com/products/shrink-packaging/poultry-shrink-bags/#:~:text=Poultry%20Shrink%20Bags%20provide%20superior

Poultry Cuts – Meat Cutting and Processing for Food Service. (n.d.). Opentextbc. https://opentextbc.ca/meatcutting/chapter/poultry-cuts/

Poultry Medication & Vaccines. (n.d.). Stromberg's Chickens. https://www.strombergschickens.com/poultry-supplies/medications-health/

Poultry Products Processing: An Industry Guide. (n.d.). Amazon. https://www.amazon.com/Poultry-Products-Processing-Industry-Guide/dp/1587160609

Quinn. (2023, January 23). *Chicken Butchering Supplies Checklist.* Reformation Acres. https://www.reformationacres.com/chicken-butchering-supplies/

Quotes about small steps. (n.d.). Bookroo. https://bookroo.com/quotes/small-steps

Rachael. (n.d.). *What Do Baby Chicks Eat? Complete Guide to Feeding Baby Chickens.* Dine a Chook. https://www.dineachook.com.au/blog/what-do-baby-chicks-eat-complete-guide-to-feeding-baby-chickens/#:~:text=Chicks%20don

Raising Chickens 101: How to Build a Chicken Coop. (2023, April 18). Old Farmer's Almanac. https://www.almanac.com/raising-chickens-101-how-build-chicken-coop

Raising happy, healthy chickens in your own backyard. (n.d.). Raising Happy Chickens. https://www.raising-happy-chickens.com/

Reddy, B. (2017, August 1). *Factors influencing the nutrient requirements of poultry.* Slide Share. https://www.slideshare.net/balakesavareddy/factors-influencing-the-nutrient-requirements-of-poultry

Remus, E. (2020, October 6). *9 Types of Chicken Feed Explained.* K&H Pet Products. https://khpet.com/blogs/farm/9-types-of-chicken-feed-explained

Reynolds, A. (2020, March 5). *The Role of Vitamins in Poultry Nutrition.* Southland Organics. https://www.southlandorganics.com/blogs/poultry-biosecurity/the-role-of-vitamins-in-poultry-nutrition#:~:text=Poultry%20requires%20all%20known%20vitamins

Rhodes, J. (2022, November 29). *Feeding Chickens Without Grain - Cut Your Costs 100%.* Abundant Permaculture. https://abundantpermaculture.com/how-to-feed-chickens-without-grain/#:~:text=Consider%20planting%20a%20grain%20crop

Ritz, C. W. (2005, August 15). *Coexisting with Neighbors: A Poultry Farmer's Guide.* The Poultry Site. https://www.thepoultrysite.com/articles/coexisting-with-neighbors-a-poultry-farmers-guide

Roberts, W. (n.d.). *Best Chicken Coop: 7 Types You Need To Know Before Buy It.* Delaney Chickens. https://delaneychicken.com/best-chicken-coop-types/

Robin. (2021, March 4). *Cornish Cross.* Burns Feed Store. https://burnsfeed.com/cornish-cross/#:~:text=Cornish%20Cross%20is%20one%20of

Robinson, A. (2021, June 30). *120 Best Hard Work Pays Off Quotes for 2021.* Team Building. https://teambuilding.com/blog/hard-work-quotes

Ryan. (n.d.). *Do chickens need a Vitamin and Mineral Supplement?* Dine a Chook. https://www.dineachook.com.au/blog/do-chickens-need-a-vitamin-and-mineral-supplement/#:~:text=Using%20a%20low%20dose%20supplement

Santopietro, J. (2018, October 9). *How to Truss a Turkey.* Epicurious. https://www.epicurious.com/expert-advice/how-to-truss-thanksgiving-turkey-easy-way-article#:~:text=Or%2C%20you%20can%20simply%20use

Sato, Y., & Wakenell, P. S. (2022, October). *Common Infectious Diseases in Backyard Poultry - Exotic and Laboratory Animals.* MSD Veterinary Manual.

https://www.msdvetmanual.com/exotic-and-laboratory-animals/backyard-poultry/common-infectious-diseases-in-backyard-poultry#v16229066

Schaible, P. J. (n.d.). *The Minerals in Poultry Nutrition--A Review*. Poultry Science. https://www.sciencedirect.com/science/article/pii/S0032579119518089#:~:text=Although%20the%20general%20functions%20of,absorption%2C%20secretion%2C%20and%20excretion.

Scratch Farmstead. (2022). You CAN Process Chickens at Home - Everything You Need to Know | Self Sufficient Homestead [Video]. YouTube. https://www.youtube.com/watch?v=zuL3vAvxVs4&list=WL&index=21&t=498s

7 Benefits to Raising Backyard Chickens. (n.d.). Strombergs. https://www.strombergschickens.com/blog/7-benefits-to-raising-backyard-chickens/

Simon. (2022, October 1). *Self Sustainability EXPLAINED*. Sustainability Success. https://sustainability-success.com/self-sustainability/#:~:text=Self%2Dsustainability%20is%20important%20for

Singh, M., Mollier, R. T., Pongener, N., Yadav, R., Vingh, V., Katiyar, R., Kunar, R., Sonia, C., Bhatt, M., Babu, S., Rajkhowa, D. J., & Mishra, V. K. (2022, October 18). *Backyard poultry farming with improved germplasm: Sustainable food production and nutritional security in fragile ecosystem (A. A. Mariod, Ed.)*. Frontiers. https://www.frontiersin.org/articles/10.3389/fsufs.2022.962268/full

62+ Best Backyard Chicken Blogs & Websites. (n.d.). Mile Four. https://milefour.com/blogs/learn/best-backyard-chicken-blogs

Smith, K. (2020a, June 16). *Chatting With Chickens – How to Communicate With Your Flock*. Backyard Chicken Coops. https://www.backyardchickencoops.com.au/blogs/learning-centre/chatting-with-chickens

Smith, K. (2020b, July 22). *Chicken Waterers 101: What You Need To Know*. Backyard Chicken Coops. https://www.backyardchickencoops.com.au/blogs/learning-centre/chicken-waterers-101-what-you-need-to-know

Smith, K. (2020c, July 22). *Why Raising Chickens Is Great For The Environment*. Backyard Chicken Coops. https://www.backyardchickencoops.com.au/blogs/learning-centre/why-raising-chickens-is-great-for-the-environment

Smtih, L. (2023, March 28). *The Basics Of Egg Incubation & Hatching Chicks*. Hobby Farms. https://www.hobbyfarms.com/the-basics-of-egg-incubation-hatching-chicks/

Sonder, T. (n.d.). *Permaculture Principle 4: Apply self-regulation & accept feedback*. Edible Evanston. https://edibleevanston.org/content/permaculture-principle-4-apply-self-regulation-accept-feedback#:~:text=Permaculture%20Principle%204%3A%20Apply%20self%2Dregulation%20%26%20accept%20feedback

Specialist Writer. (2022, October 26). *Poultry farming part 7: Record keeping*. ProAgri. https://proagri.co.za/poultry-farming-part-7-record-keeping/#:~:text=Daily%20information%20must%20be%20recorded

Spice, C. (2021, January 13). *Cage-Free vs. Free-Range vs. Organic Eggs: The Difference Between Egg Labels*. Colorado Spice. https://coloradospice.-

com/blogs/news/cage-free-vs-organic-eggs#:~:text=Under%20the%20US-DA%20Organic%20Certification

St. Cyr, K. (2022, August 12). *Pros and Cons of Red Ranger Chickens vs. Cornish Cross Chickens - Backyard Poultry.* Backyard Poultry. https://backyardpoultry.iam-countryside.com/eggs-meat/red-ranger-chickens-vs-cornish-cross-chickens/

Standard Chicken Coop - Made In USA. (n.d.). The Shed Yard. https://theshedyard.com/standard-chicken-coop/

Steele, L. (n.d.). *Will Raising Chickens for Eggs Really Save You Money?* Fresh Eggs Daily. https://www.fresheggsdaily.blog/2022/07/will-raising-chickens-for-eggs-really.html#:~:text=The%20simple%20answer%20is%2C%20initially

Stoney Ridge Farmer. (2019). The Easy Way to Process and Butcher Chicken [Video]. YouTube. https://www.youtube.com/watch?v=FzCMgmyBeZI

Stoney Ridge Farmer. (n.d.). [YouTube channel]. YouTube. https://www.youtube.com/@StoneyRidgeFarmer/videos

Storey's Illustrated Guide to Poultry Breeds: Chickens, Ducks, Geese, Turkeys, Emus, Guinea Fowl, Ostriches, Partridges, Peafowl, Pheasants, Quails, Swans. (n.d.). Amazon. https://www.amazon.com/Storeys-Illustrated-Guide-Poultry-Breeds/dp/1580176674

Strauss, E. (n.d.). *Permaculture Chicken Keeping.* Hobby Farms. https://www.hobby-farms.com/permaculture-chicken-keeping/

Successful cleaning and hygiene for butchers. (n.d.). Kärcher International. https://www.kaercher.com/int/professional/know-how/cleaning-for-butchers.html#:~:text=Alkaline%20detergents%20(pH%208%2D14

Suscovich, J. (2016). How to Kill a Chicken Humanely (Graphic) [Video]. YouTube. https://www.youtube.com/watch?v=1K6e8Fisq7Q

Swan, S. (n.d.). *From Chickens to Hope.* Episcopal Relief & Development. https://www.episcopalrelief.org/stories/from-chickens-to-hope/

Tejeda, O. J., & Kim, W. K. (2021). Role of Dietary Fiber in Poultry Nutrition. *Animals, 11*(2), 461. https://doi.org/10.3390/ani11020461

The Behavioural Biology of Chickens. (n.d.). Amazon. https://www.amazon.com/Behavioural-Biology-Chickens-Christina-Nicol/dp/1780642504

The benefits of using an automatic egg incubator. (2021, November 2). River Systems. https://www.riversystems.it/en/benefits-uses-incubators-eggs/

The Best Egg Laying Chickens: A Guide to Egg Production . (n.d.). IFA. https://grow.ifa.coop/chickens/best-egg-laying-chickens#:~:text=How%20Many%20Eggs%20Do%20Chickens

The Cornish Cross Chicken. (2022, March 15). The Happy Chicken Coop. https://www.thehappychickencoop.com/the-cornish-cross-chicken/

The Editors. (2023, July 3). *Raising Chickens 101: Collecting, Cleaning, Storing, Hatching Eggs!* The Old Farmer's Almanac. https://www.almanac.com/raising-chickens-101-collecting-storing-and-hatching-chicken-eggs#:~:text=Ideal-ly%2C%20wait%20until%20the%20hens

The Farm That Feeds Us: A Year in the Life of an Organic Farm. (n.d.). Goodreads.

Retrieved   August   8,   2023,   from
https://www.goodreads.com/en/book/show/51349850

The Galloway Farm. (2022). STEP BY STEP: BUTCHERING + PROCESSING MEAT
CHICKENS! [Video]. YouTube. https://www.youtube.com/watch?v=_rn0pfc-
qnS0&list=WL&index=23&t=569s

The Hidden Lives of Chickens. (n.d.). PETA. https://www.peta.org/issues/animals-
used-for-food/factory-farming/chickens/hidden-lives-chick-
ens/#:~:text=Some%20are%20gregarious%20and%20fearless

The REAL best chicken breeds for hot climates: NOT what you've been told. (n.d.). The
Featherbrain.   https://www.thefeatherbrain.com/blog/hot-climate-chicken-
breeds#:~:text=Some%20of%20your%20Brahmas%20and

The Spruce - Make Your Best Home. (n.d.). The Spruce. https://www.thespruce.com/

Theresa. (n.d.). *Freezing Food.* Our Tiny Homestead. https://www.ourtinyhome-
stead.com/freezing-food.html

Thesing, G. (2017, September 13). *Chicken Predators – What You Need to Know.* The
Scoop from the Coop. https://www.scoopfromthecoop.com/chicken-predators-
what-you-need-to-know/#:~:text=Most%20chicken%20losses%20occur%20at

THIAMIN DEFICIENCY IN PULLETS. (n.d.). Technical Update. https://www.hy-
line.com/ViewFile?id=90674bcd-35c8-4b8d-a337-34373a04ce39#:~:text=Thi-
amin%2C%20also%20known%20as%20vitamin

3   Best   Chicken   Breeds   to   Raise   for   Meat. (n.d.).   Strombergs.
https://www.strombergschickens.com/blog/3-best-chicken-breeds-to-raise-for-
meat/

Tips for Housing & Outdoor Space for Chickens. (n.d.). RSPCA. https://www.rsp-
ca.org.uk/adviceandwelfare/farm/farmanimals/chickens/environ-
ment#:~:text=Chickens%20need%20a%20warm%2C%20dry

Tom. (n.d.). *To Build Or Buy A Chicken Coop, That Is The Question - Free Chicken Coop
Plans.* Free Chicken Coop Plans. https://freechickencoopplans.com/to-build-or-
buy-a-chicken-coop-that-is-the-question/

Toney, S. (2022, October 4). *Chicken Coop Necessities: 6 Things Your Coop Must Have.*
The Free Range Life. https://thefreerangelife.com/chicken-coop-necessities/

TOP 25 PERMACULTURE QUOTES. (n.d.). A-Z Quotes. https://www.azquotes.-
com/quotes/topics/permaculture.html#:~:text=The%20only%20ethical%20de-
cision%20is

TOP   25   SELF   SUFFICIENT   QUOTES   (of   138). (n.d.).   A-Z   Quotes.
https://www.azquotes.com/quotes/topics/self-sufficient.html

Twain, L. (2022, June 20). *What To Know Before Building Your Own Chicken Coop.* The
Scoop   from   the   Coop.   https://www.scoopfromthecoop.com/what-to-know-
before-building-your-own-chicken-coop/

Types of Fat. (n.d.). Harvard T. H. Chan. https://www.hsph.harvard.edu/nutrition-
source/what-should-you-eat/fats-and-cholesterol/types-of-fat/#:~:text=Unsat-
urated%20fats%2C%20which%20are%20liquid

Ukraine war: What are the impacts on the world today?. (2022, August 23). International

Rescue Committee. https://www.rescue.org/article/ukraine-war-what-are-impacts-world-today#:~:text=The%20continued%20conflict%20in%20Ukraine

Valls, J. B. (2021, July 1). *Relationship between nutrition and genetics in poultry production.* Veterinaria Digital. https://www.veterinariadigital.com/en/articulos/relationship-between-nutrition-and-genetics-in-poultry-production/

Van der Linden, C. (2022, February 25). *Which Items Are "Greens" and Which Are "Browns" for Composting?* The Spruce. https://www.thespruce.com/composting-greens-and-browns-2539485#:~:text=The%20Compost%20Ratio&text=Generally%2C%20a%20ratio%20of%203

Van Eden, D. (2021, March 30). *Permaculture: 12 principles to farm like Mother Nature.* Food for Mzanzi. https://www.foodformzansi.co.za/12-principles-of-permaculture/

Vest, L., & Dale, N. (2022, July 7). *Nutrition for the Backyard Flock.* University of Georgia. https://extension.uga.edu/publications/detail.html?number=C954&title=nutrition-for-the-backyard-flock#:~:text=Carbohydrates%20are%20used%20as%20a

Waddington, E. (2019, April 23). *The 12 Principles of Permaculture: A Way Forward.* Earth Fm. https://earth.fm/earth-stories/permaculture-principles/

Wayment, H., Shupe, S., Goodrich, M., & Singleton, J. (n.d.). *What To Feed Your Chickens From Chicks To Egg-Laying Hens.* IFA. https://grow.ifa.coop/chickens/what-to-feed-your-chickens-from-chicks-to-hens

West, H. (2021, June 13). *Egg Whites Nutrition: High in Protein, Low in Everything Else.* Healthline. https://www.healthline.com/nutrition/egg-whites-nutrition#Low-in-calories-but-high-in-protein

What are the 4 types of poultry housing Archives? (n.d.). POULTRY MANIA. https://poultrymania.com/tag/what-are-the-4-types-of-poultry-housing/

What do Baby Chicks Eat? - Backyard Chicken Advice. (2017, February 9). Chicken Coops and Tractors Australia. https://www.thechickentractor.com.au/what-do-baby-chicks-eat/#:~:text=Teaching%20Chicks%20to%20Eat%20and%20Drink&text=This%20can%20be%20done%20easily

What is a chicken run? (2022, October 11). My Pet Chicken. https://www.mypetchicken.com/blogs/faqs/what-is-a-chicken-run

What is the Best Wire Mesh for a Chicken Run? (n.d.). TWP. https://www.twpinc.com/blog/what-is-the-best-wire-for-chicken-run.html

What is your carbon footprint? (n.d.). The Nature Conservancy. https://www.nature.org/en-us/get-involved/how-to-help/carbon-footprint-calculator/

What the Hen? The Difference Between Broilers & Laying Hens. (2020, November 1). Organic Alberta. https://organicalberta.org/article/what-the-hen-the-difference-between-broilers-laying-hens

Which chicken breeds may need extra heat in winter? (2022, October 11). My Pet Chicken. https://www.mypetchicken.com/blogs/faqs/which-chicken-breeds-may-need-extra-heat-in-winter

White, J. (2014, December 14). *DIY Chicken Coops: The Complete Guide To Building Your Own Chicken Coop.* Amazon.

Why blanch? (n.d.). Clemson University, South Carolina. https://www.clemson.edu/extension/food/canning/canning-tips/43why-blanch.html#:~:text=Blanching%20stops%20enzyme%20actions%20which

Wiley. (2017, May 5). *Poultry feed with arsenic more problematic than assumed? New methylated phenylarsenical metabolites identified in chicken livers.* Science Daily. https://www.sciencedaily.com/releases/2017/05/170505103620.htm#:~:text=Supplements%20containing%20arsenic%20have%20been

Willis, K., & Ludlow, R. T. (2016, March 26). *Packaging Home-Butchered Poultry.* Dummies. https://www.dummies.com/article/home-auto-hobbies/hobby-farming/chickens/packaging-home-butchered-poultry-145313/

Winger, J. (n.d.). *Return to your roots.* The Prairie Homestead. https://www.theprairiehomestead.com/

Winger, J. (2020, May 28). *How to Butcher a Chicken.* The Prairie Homestead. https://www.theprairiehomestead.com/2016/07/how-to-butcher-a-chicken.html

Winger, J. (2023a, June 30). *Canning Chicken (How to do it Safely).* The Prairie Homestead. https://www.theprairiehomestead.com/2020/03/canning-chicken.html

Winger, J. (2023b, June 30). *My Favorite Ways to Preserve Food at Home.* The Prairie Homestead. https://www.theprairiehomestead.com/2020/08/ways-to-preserve-food-at-home.html

World Economic Situation and Prospects as of mid-2023. (2023, May 16). United Nations. https://www.un.org/development/desa/dpad/publication/world-economic-situation-and-prospects-as-of-mid-2023/#:~:text=Global%20trade%20remains%20under%20pressure

Wyss, L. (2020, December 28). *How To Humanely Kill A Chicken.* Insteading. https://insteading.com/blog/chicken-slaughter/

Young, M. (n.d.). *5 Best Containers for Small Scale Egg Producers.* Farm Fit Living. https://farmfitliving.com/5-best-egg-containers-for-small-scale-egg-producers/

Your health. (n.d.). Compassion in World Farming. https://www.ciwf.org.uk/factory-farming/your-health/#:~:text=Food%2Dborne%20illnesses